to exploring the
Lizard Peninsula

including
Coverack Porthallow
Mullion Cadgwith
Porthleven
St Keverne
&
The complete coastal footpath & circular inland walks, many ending in a pub

Friendly Guide
• *First Edition* •

Safety by the Sea

Every year fatalities occur around the coast because people ignore simple & common sense rules when they are by the sea. NEVER take the sea for granted.

Do not swim after a meal or after consuming alcohol.

Never swim off headlands - strong currents can pull you out to sea even on a calm day.

Do not let children go into the sea on an air bed or inflatable - they can quickly be drawn out to sea by offshore winds or on a riptide.

Never touch strange objects washed up by the sea - dangerous canisters containing flares, munitions & chemicals are sometimes brought ashore. If you find something suspicious inform the Coastguard or Police.

ALWAYS obey lifeguards - they are aware of dangers that may not be apparent to you.

Never approach the edge of a cliff - it may be unstable or slippery.

If you are exploring a cliff base be aware of the tide and unstable cliffs above you.

Do not sit or walk close to rocks that are being swept by waves - an unexpectedly large wave can pull you into the sea.

Be aware of other people who may be in danger. If in doubt, telephone 999 and ask for the Coastguard - you may save a life.

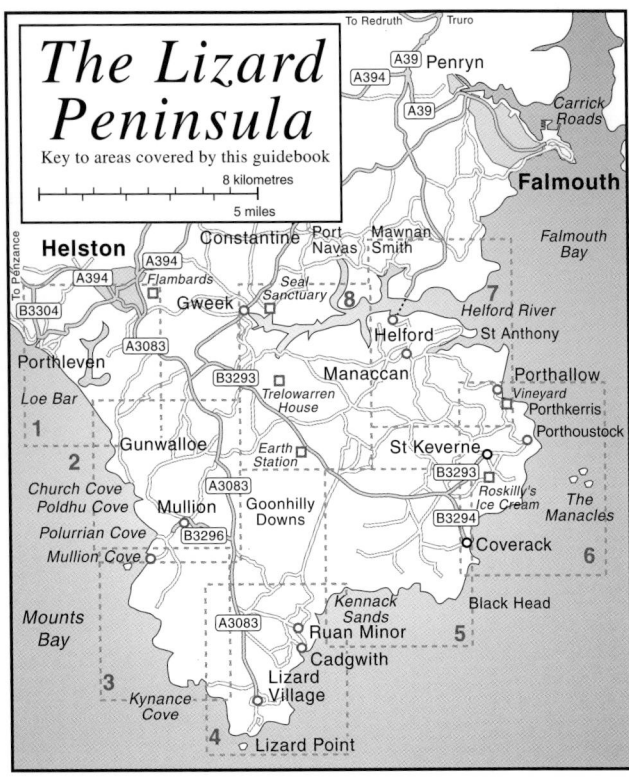

Published by Cormorant Design
PENZANCE
Cornwall
Telephone (01736) 369194
© Neil Reid 1999
ISBN 0 9520874 5 6

The Publishers gratefully acknowledge the help and cooperation of the National Trust in the production of this guidebook.

Picture Credits
Watercolour illustrations by Bridgitte Livesley. Tel.: 0171 737 7773
Andrew Besley - front cover, p25: Paul Watts - back cover, pp4, 8, 16(top & bottom), 29(bottom), 37, 40, 41, 44 & 45; Frank Gibson - pp15, 31(top) & 31(bottom); National Trust p12 (top), National Trust/JS Gifford p12 (bottom), National Trust/Andrew Besley p13(top), National Trust p13 (bottom), National Trust p17(bottom), National Trust/DJ Flunder p24, National Trust/Andrew Besley p29(top).

Every possible care has been taken to ensure that the information shown in this guide is accurate and whilst the Publishers would be grateful to learn of any errors, they regret they can accept no responsibility for any expense, loss or injury caused as a consequence. The accuracy of any information in adverts is the sole responsibility of the advertiser.

Contents

Beach Guide	4
Things to do	6
Introduction	7
Geology, Landscape and Wildlife of the Lizard	8
People of the Lizard	14
1. Porthleven & Loe Bar	15

Walk 1. *A walk around Loe Pool.*
Long circular walk which can be easily divided into smaller sections.

2. Gunwalloe, Poldhu & Mullion	19

Walk 2. *A circular walk from Mullion.*
Cliff walk between some of the best beaches on the Lizard.

3. Mullion Cove & Kynance Cove	23

Walk 3. *Mullion Cove & Predannack cliff.*
High cliffs leading down to Ogo-dour Cove. National Nature Reserve
Stroll. *A stroll around Kynance Cove.*
Ever popular beauty spot. Check the tide is out before you go.

4. Lizard Point & Cadgwith	27

Walk 4. *A circular walk from Lizard Point to Church Cove.*
Popular coastal walk past Lizard Lighthouse & the Lion's Den.
Stroll. *A stroll around Lizard Point.*
Easy stroll to the derelict lifeboat station below Lizard Point. Good sea views

Shipwrecks Around the Lizard	31
5. Kennack Sands	32

Walk 5. *A cliff walk from Kennack Sands to Downas Cove.*

6. Coverack, St Keverne & The Manacles	35

Walk 6. *A long circular walk from St Keverne to Porthallow.*
Great combination walk through beautiful valleys & onto the cliffs.

7. St Anthony, Manaccan & Helford Village	39

Walk 7. *A walk around Rosemullion Head (via ferry).*
Peaceful walk with views over to Falmouth Bay. Visit gardens & pubs.
Stroll. *A stroll to Frenchman's Creek from Helford Village.*

8. Gweek, Trelowarren & Goonhilly	43

Walk 8. *Trelowarren Woodland Walk (Easter to October).*
Stroll. *A stroll to Tremayne Quay.*
Wander down to the banks of the Helford river.

Glossary of Geological terms	47
Rocks of the Lizard	48

Beach Guide

Church Cove, Gunwalloe. Perfect family beach

Information
Helston & The Lizard TIC, 79 Meneage Street, Helston.
Tel. 01326 565431
The Lizard Countryside Centre, Trelowarren. Tel. 01326 221661

Banks
Helston has branches of all four major banks and most of the national building societies. Cash tills are also available at Tesco superstore in Helston. Mullion has branches of Lloyds & Barclays banks (open Tuesday & Thursday).

Beach Guide

Warning flags at the beach

- Bathing safe between flags
- No swimming - area between flags reserved for surfing, canoeing and other water sports.
- No swimming - hazardous conditions
- Area between flags reserved for the landing of craft

Almost all of the really good beaches on the Lizard are on the west coast of the peninsular starting at Gunwalloe & ending at Mullion Cove. They have golden sand and are of course, very popular. The only other similar sandy beach is Kennack Sands on the east coast which is a wonderful beach. The other beaches on the sheltered east coast are more pebbly but can be gloriously empty such as Godrevy beach near St Keverne. Otherwise there are numerous small coves around the coast which are readily accessible & never crowded. They can be discovered by simply setting off along the coast path with a picnic. Best beaches for families - Gunwalloe, Poldhu, Polurrian or Kennack Sands; for drama - Mullion Cove; for tranquillity - Grebe beach on the north bank of the Helford & for shear holiday heaven Passage Cove with a pub above the beach & rock pools for the kids.

Porthleven - East Beach
Sandy beach just outside the harbour wall. Swimming dangerous at low tide or in rough conditions.

Loe Bar
Steeply shelving beach combined with extremely dangerous currents and freak waves even on calm days, mean that nobody in their right mind ever swims here - whatever the conditions.

Gunwalloe - Church Cove
Perfect family beach. Plenty of sand even at high water with a stream for small children to play in. Small cafe sells refreshments and pasties. Search for Spanish treasure from a wrecked ship at Dollar Cove. Park in large National Trust car park above Winnianton Farm.

The Haven

Bed & Breakfast
Guests Lounge, colour TV.
Centre of village, close to
Cornish coastal footpath,
ideal centre for walkers,
dogs welcome.

Ruan Minor, Helston, Cornwall. TR12 7JL
Tel: (01326) 290410   Contact Denise Wilson

Please mention this guidebook when replying to advertisements

Dogs allowed all year. Other beaches dogs banned Easter to Oct.

Poldhu Cove
Large sandy beach with cafe & large car park. Good cliff walks on either side of the cove.

Polurrian Cove
Large sandy beach. Nearest parking is in Mullion Village about 10 minutes walk from beach.

Mullion Cove
Wide expanse of sand only exposed a low tide. Accessible via tunnel from Mullion Cove harbour. Perfect for cricket & football and perfectly set against high cliffs of dark serpentine. Car park, cafe & toilets at Mullion Cove harbour.

Kynance Cove
Really a beach for exploring rather than swimming. Numerous islands & wonderful caves with polished walls of serpentine. Be aware of the tide as one can easily become stranded. Park in National Trust car park 5 minutes walk from cove. Refreshments at car park, cafe at cove.

Pentreath Beach
Sand only at low water. Less crowded than Kynance. No facilities.

Housel Cove
Small beach at foot of cliffs. Moderately difficult decent. Housel Bay Hotel above cove provides bar snacks and meals all year.

Cadgwith Cove
Small beach covered at high water. Pub, toilet and shops above beach. No dogs on western beach.

Kennack Sands
Wonderful family beach with golden sand, streams and rock pools. Large car park, cafe, shop & toilets. Dogs on eastern beach only.

Coverack
Good beach for playing football. Gentle walk to Lowland Point. All facilities in Coverack.

Leggan & Godrevy Cove
Wonderfully deserted pebbly beaches. Extremely limited roadside parking at Rosenithon or park above Polcries Cove.

Porthoustock Cove
Pebbly beach sandwiched between quarries. Mostly used by divers.

Porthallow Cove
Pebbly beach easily accessible from large beach car park. Five Pilchards pub, cafes & other facilities nearby.

Gillan Beach
Small sandy beach much used by yachtsmen. Quiet, no facilities.

Bosahan Cove
The first of three tiny hidden sandy beaches on the coast path between St Anthony and Helford Village. Park at St Anthony, no facilities, may lose sun in late afternoon. No dogs allowed on coast path here.

Passage Cove
Small sandy beach on north side of Helford River. Good for taking children as getting there from the Lizard side involves taking the pedestrian ferry from Helford Village (check ferry times on 01326 250278). Parents can sit and sip cocktails in the Ferry Boat Inn and still be able to supervise children on the beach. Short walk east to the sub tropical gardens of Trebah and Glendurgan.

Grebe Beach
One of the best small beaches in Cornwall and a bit of a secret - 10 minutes walk from Helford Passage. National Trust car park at top of hill above beach. No facilities.

TRURONIAN

LOCAL BUS SERVICES TRURONIAN OPERATE ON THE LIZARD

Service T1 Perranporth - St Agnes- Truro - Helston - Mullion - The Lizard with new EASY ACCESS BUSES (Mondays to Saturdays and Sundays in the summer) *serving Flambards Theme Park*

Service T2 Helston - Coverack and St Keverne, with connections to Truro (Mondays to Saturdays) *serving Goonhilly Earth Satellite Station*

Service T3 -The Lizard Rambler Helston - Mawgan - St Martin - Helford Village - Manaccan - Porthallow - St Keverne - Tregellast Barton - Coverack - Ruan Minor - Kynance Cove (Mon-Sat and Sundays in the summer) *serving Roskilly's*

Service T4 Helston to Falmouth (Mondays to Saturdays and Sundays in the summer) *serving Gweek, Trebah/Glendurgan Gardens & Helford Passage*

For information tel. Truronian Buses (01872) 273453

Please mention this guidebook when replying to advertisements

Beach patrolled by life guard

Things to Do

The Lizard Countryside Centre See Section 8.
At Trelowarren House (see below) - the best introduction to the geology, archaeology and wildlife of the Lizard Peninsula & the perfect way to get your bearings at the start of your visit.

[T3] Frenchman's Creek See Sections 7 & 8.
Sublime tiny creek on the Helford river. Supposedly the setting for the romantic canoodling in Daphne du Maurier's novel of the same name. Reached by footpath from Helford Village (1½ mile round trip). Best visited early morning or late evening ending in the Shipwrights pub in Helford Village.

[T1] Lizard Point See Section 4.
The most southerly point in the UK. Wonderful in gales as the waves break over the Man-of-War reef. Concrete road leads to the derelict lifeboat house in Polpeor Cove.

[T3] Kynance Cove See Section 3.
Famous beauty spot. Reached by road from the A3083 on Lizard Downs or by footpath from Lizard Town. Best visited at low water when the islands become accessible. Likely to be busy in the summer school holidays. Cafe above cove.

Trelowarren House See Section 8.
Lizard Countryside Centre (see above), Cornwall Craft Association Gallery, bistro & pottery. Woodland walks during the season.

Goonhilly Earth Station See Section 8.
State-of-the-art satellite station in wonderful contrast with the bleak, wildness of Goonhilly Downs. Handles millions of phone calls a year. Visitor centre, children's adventure playground, surf the Internet.

[T1] Flambards Theme Park See Section 1.
The best funfair in Cornwall with roller coaster ride & static displays of helicopters and aircraft from the adjacent naval air base. Good rides for smaller children. Very busy in school holidays especially on overcast days. Reduced entry fee in the afternoon.

[T3] Roskilly's Ice Cream See Section 6.
Ice cream to die for - made on the farm with milk from their own cows. Watch milking every afternoon. Wildlife trail follows the valley down to Godrevy Cove, once the home to the notorious footpads & smugglers of the Long Meadow Gang.

[T4] Trebah & Glendurgan Gardens See Section 7.
Famous sub tropical gardens on the north bank of the Helford. Take the pedestrian ferry from Helford Village. Trebah Garden open every day of the year. Glendurgan open Tues.-Sat, March-October.

[T4] National Seal Sanctuary, Gweek See Section 8.
Hospital for hurt & damaged seals and seal pups. Most are returned to the wild on their recovery. Permanent residents include sealions. Best time to visit is feeding time. Open every day. Cafe & shop. For more information telephone (01326) 221361.

Wreck Diving & Boat Trips
Diving tuition for novices at Porthkerris Cove. Dive on wrecks on the Manacles Reef. Boat trips leave from Cadgwith & Mullion in the summer to view the coast, watch seals & for fishing trips.

Boat hire & sailing tuition
From St Anthony on Carne Creek at the mouth of the Helford river - tel. (01326) 231357; & from Helford Passage - tel. (01326) 250770.

Pubs with a sea view
Pubs where you can sit out with a view over the ocean.
Ship Inn, Porthleven; *Halzephron Inn*, Gunwalloe; *Cove Hotel*, Cadgwith (Cornish songs on a Friday night); *Paris Hotel*, Coverack; *Five Pilchards*, Porthallow; *Shipwrights Arms*, Helford Village; *Ferry Boat Inn*, Helford Passage (via foot ferry from Helford Village).

Best thing to do if it rains
Take a creekside walk in the woods or walk by the sea - for the sake of your own sanity avoid all tourist attractions on rainy days as they become extremely crowded. The sea always looks beautiful in the rain. Try the strolls to Tremayne Quay or Frenchman's Creek.

Introduction

The wonderful thing about exploring the Lizard Peninsula is that the rocks and the landscape exposed here allow one to leap the divide between the ordinary human scale of space and time, and the greater geological scale. In this remote part of Cornwall Mother Nature has reluctantly given up rocks that are rarely exposed to the human eye and properly make up the core of our planet. Perhaps this is why one always has a feeling of excitement and expectancy as one drives towards the Lizard. The whole peninsula has a distinctive and exotic quality that makes it feel quite different to other parts of Cornwall. It is almost as if when one enters the Lizard one unknowingly passes through a looking glass into a landscape at once familiar, with all the usual hills and coves, but at the same time quite tangibly different in character.

One reason for its distinctiveness must be because the Lizard is so physically isolated, being surrounded on all sides by water. The only land link with the rest of Cornwall is the watershed between the wooded valleys of the **Helford river** that flows east into Falmouth Bay, and the Carnminowe stream which flows west to **Loe Pool**. Having passed along this thin spine one finds oneself not in the characteristic Cornish landscape of rolling slate hills and craggy granite uplands, but in a landscape where this geology has been substituted by a medley of unusual rocks.

The key to the character of the Lizard lies in its unusual geology. At the centre of the peninsula is an area of inhospitable ancient heath almost untouched and uncultivated by man. This bleak area which comprises **Goonhilly, Predannack** and **Lizard Downs** corresponds with the outcrop of a rock called *serpentine*. The texture and colour of serpentine rock can mimic the skin of a lizard, and thus has given its name to the whole peninsula. This rock forms the huge volume of the mantle below the thin outer crust of the earth. Very occasionally it is ripped from the mantle by earth movements and exposed at the surface. The geology hints at a much larger picture. It illustrates processes that create and destroy whole continents and that have been continuously shaping our planet for billions of years.

The rocks that surround the serpentine such as *schist* and *gabbro* form unusually deep and fertile soils that will nourish almost any seed a farmer cares to scatter. This is in contrast to the serpentine which forms a waterlogged and unwilling clay. The division between these rocks and the serpentine is often very clear and sharp. The vegetation may completely change within a few metres from lush pasture to windblown heath and this tends to reinforce the sense of strangeness that one sometimes feels on the Lizard. Even within the context of Cornwall the Lizard stands out as different. The harder you look, the more captivated you become by the unusual, varied and beautiful landscapes that exist here.

Roskilly's

Do come and visit the farm for:-
EXCELLENT ICE CREAMS MADE ON THE FARM
Super SALADS, SOUPS & PIZZAS
Delicious HOME-MADE CREAM TEAS
WALKS round the PONDS & MEADOWS
WATCH MILKING 4.30-5.30
OPEN ALL DAY   FREE PARKING

Tregellast Barton, $^1/_2$ mile South of St Keverne. Tel. 01326 280479

Please mention this guidebook when replying to advertisements

Geology, Landscape & Wildlife

Goonhilly Downs & Earth Station. The serpentine rock forms an unusual & rare habitat. Cornish heath thrives on the poor, wet soils which are also a haven to reptiles & amphibians.

The rocks of the Lizard are thought to represent rocks usually found in a vertical sequence in the earth's oceanic crust - the portion of the earth that reaches down about seven kilometres from the sea bed to the mantle - the outer part of the earth's core. This typical sequence of rocks is called an *ophiolite* and is occasionally torn from the mantle and thrust onto the surface by huge and prolonged earth movements. The different rocks of the ophiolite come from the same source - the mantle, but they become altered in their passage to the surface. The type

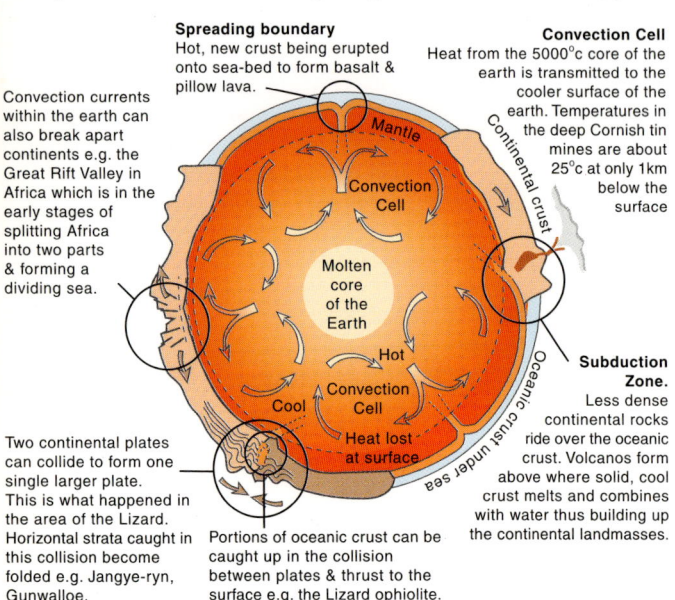

Fig. 1. Schematic section through the earth illustrating how movement at the earths surface is generated from within the planet.

of rock they change into depends on varying factors such as how rapidly they cool and what contact they have with other chemicals on their passage from the mantle to the surface. For instance, molten rock from the mantle erupted onto the sea floor is very rapidly chilled and its chemical composition is altered as it comes into contact with sea water. The typical type of rock formed at the sea bed is a hard *basalt* or *pillow lava*. **Mullion Island** is composed of pillow lava. Molten magma that does not make it to the surface will cool much more slowly to form large crystalline rocks such as *gabbro*. The *serpentine* rock which forms over half the area of the Lizard, is rarely seen at the surface because it constitutes the source rock in the mantle and it can only reach the surface in its unaltered state, if it has already solidified many kilometres underground and is then physically plucked from there by earth movements.

From the geological perspective the surface of the earth is in constant motion. The rocks of the mantle behave in a semi-fluid way distributing heat from the hot, molten core of the

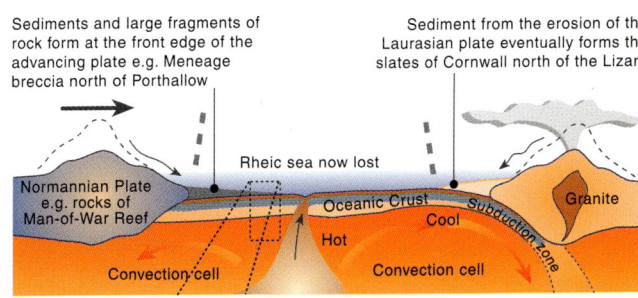

Fig. 2. Schematic section through the area that will eventually form the Lizard illustrating the origin of some of the main rocks.

We know from the observation of seismic waves caused by earthquakes that the earth is not composed of a uniform material. Seismic waves will change their speed as they pass through different layers within the earth. From this observation geologists have established there is an outer layer of crust about 7km deep under the oceans & about 40km deep beneath the continents. The first boundary - called the MoHo is where the waves increase their speed.

The rocks of the Lizard originally formed part of the **oceanic crust** under a now lost sea. Three distinct & typical layers can be identified in oceanic crust.

Firstly, a thin covering of ash deposited from volcanic eruptions & fine silt sediment from the erosion of rocks on land & carried by rivers to the sea floor. Within this deep sea ooze live tiny animals called radiolaria with skeletons of silicon. The remains of these skeletons eventually form the rocks *flint & chert* - abundant on **Loe Bar**. Also, sometimes a layer of jumbled rock debris called *breccia* deposited in front of an advancing continent - the **Meneage breccia** north of **Porthallow**.

Secondly, a layer of fine grained volcanic rock that has cooled quickly such as the *pillow lava* of **Mullion Island** which was erupted onto the sea floor & later covered with sediment. Below that, a series of vertical sheets which have cooled rapidly after being injected into fractures caused by the spreading of the sea floor e.g. *basalt & greenstone* at **Manacle Point**. These dykes feed the pillow lava.

Thirdly, a layer of coarse grained igneous rock that has cooled slowly underground e.g. the *gabbro* on the east of the Lizard between **Porthoustock** & **Coverack**.

The MoHo is the boundary between the crust & the mantle. Below the crust are the rocks of the mantle e.g. *serpentine* at **Kynance Cove**. The rocks are very hot (1,000°C) & dense. They are kept solid because of the weight of rock above but are able to slowly move in a fluid way. This sounds impossible, but apparently solid materials such as glass will flow over time. Georgian window panes are noticeably thicker at their base. If the pressure above the mantle rocks is released they become liquid.

Fig. 3. Schematic section through oceanic crust & mantle to illustrate the positions where rocks of the Lizard were formed.

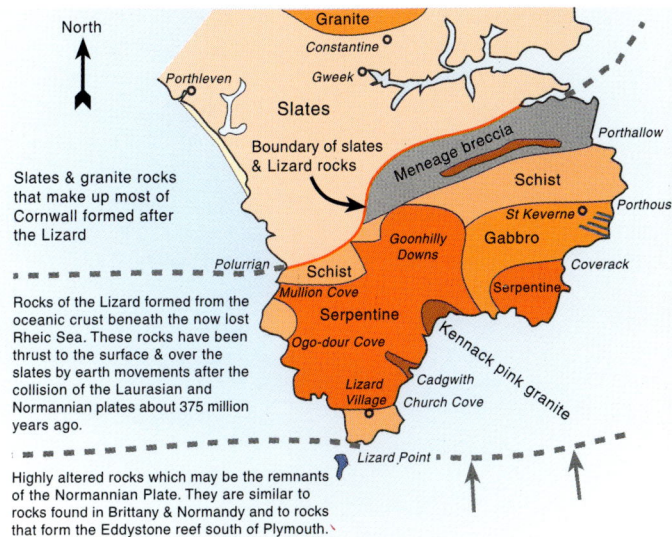

Slates & granite rocks that make up most of Cornwall formed after the Lizard

Rocks of the Lizard formed from the oceanic crust beneath the now lost Rheic Sea. These rocks have been thrust to the surface & over the slates by earth movements after the collision of the Laurasian and Normannian plates about 375 million years ago.

Highly altered rocks which may be the remnants of the Normannian Plate. They are similar to rocks found in Brittany & Normandy and to rocks that form the Eddystone reef south of Plymouth.

Fig. 4. The rocks of the Lizard Peninsula

earth to the cooler, surface of the planet. A movement is set up within the mantle where hot, and therefore less dense rock rises, and cooler, denser rock sinks. This form of heat distribution is called a *convection cell* and is active throughout the universe at every level. In our atmosphere this mechanism is commonly known as 'the weather' and it is the same mechanism that cools a cup of tea. As a result of this fluid movement the solid surface crust of the earth is broken up into seven huge crustal plates 'floating' above the mantle. The continents, which constitute the dry land part of the crust are then propelled around the surface of the earth by the movement of the convection cell. This geological process, which acts over many millions of years is called *continental drift*. We experience the motion of the continents in human space and time as earthquakes when the earth's solid crust fractures and moves, sometimes by as much as two or three metres at a time.

Since the formation of our planet about $4^1/_2$ billion years ago the shape of the crustal plates has changed as the fluid convection cells within the planet change direction. The plates are constantly jostling with one another, sometimes smashing into each other to form mountain ranges and single super-continents, and sometimes sliding past each other as at the San Andreas fault in California. Others will break apart into smaller sections as convection cells well up beneath them. In this way rocks formed in the southern hemisphere can be transported by continental drift to the northern hemisphere. Analysis of the rocks of Cornwall has shown some were formed at a position near the equator and have since been driven north by continental drift. The enormous pressures and strains of movement can also be expressed in the rocks themselves - sedimentary rocks laid down as horizontal layers can be squeezed into tight vertical folds in a sort of ultra slow motion crash (this can be seen in the folded slates at **Jangye-ryn beach** near **Gunwalloe**).

The Lizard appears to lie in the collision zone between two ancient continental plates - the Normannian Plate to the south and the Laurasian Plate to the north. They became fused together about 375 million years ago. The oceanic crust that originally divided them was mostly overridden but a portion of the crust caught in this collision seems to have become thrust up to the surface of the earth. This is the sequence of rocks that make up the larger part of the Lizard (fig. 3). The schist rocks that surround the ophiolite represent silt and sediment laid down on the sea floor but which have been altered by the intense pressures of the earth movements which brought the ophiolite to the surface. Rocks of the southern Laurasian plate are represented by the rocks of the **Man-of-War** reef off **Lizard Point**. They are very similar to rocks found in Normandy and Brittany and therefore thought to be part of the same plate and are possibly as much as 600 million years old. The original rocks of the Laurasian plate are not visible but the slates that make up the northern boundary of the Lizard are thought to be formed at least in part from sediment resulting from the erosion of the Laurasian mountains.

The *Meneage breccia* is a mile wide band of debris that makes up over half of the northern boundary of the Lizard. It is composed of a mush of different rock types some of which are not known to outcrop locally but are assumed to be remnants accumulated in front of the Normannian plate as it pushed north (fig 2). They contain large rafts of quartzite a rock similar in age to the rocks of the Man-of-War reef.

Landscape

One of the lovely things about exploring the coves and downs of the Lizard is the way in which the relationship between the bedrocks and the landscape is so clearly visible. For instance, the sea will erode the weak joint between differing rocks to form a cove. So it is that on the Lizard almost every cove conveniently marks the junction between different rock types. At **Poldhu Cove** you find a boundary between the slates of Cornwall and the schists of the Lizard; at **Mullion Cove** the boundary between the schists and the serpentine; at **Coverack** the boundary between the serpentine and gabbro and so on around the whole coastline. This makes the Lizard Peninsula coastline the most varied in Cornwall as each rock type forms a characteristic coastal scenery. The serpentine forms the highest cliffs because it is the most resistant rock having been forged in the centre of the earth. Hence it forms the dark emerald cliffs south of **Mullion Cove** and the 90 metre high cliffs of **Vellan Head**. The slates, weakened by intense deformation, form an indented coast of low cliffs like those at **Gunwalloe** and the rolling landscape of **The Meneage**. Faults or cracks within any type of rock are attacked and eroded by the sea to form deep caves. These caves often become homes for seals, particularly on the west coast beyond **Lizard Head**. Where the roofs of the caves become unstable they can collapse to form hollows and holes such as the **Devil's Frying Pan** south of **Cadgwith**, and **The Lion's Den** near **Lizard Point**.

Inland, the boundaries between the rocks are less obvious as the whole peninsula was planed flat when the rocks were part of an ancient sea-bed 200 million years ago. Subsequent erosion by wind and rain has eroded valleys in the rocks surrounding the serpentine. Where pink granite replaces the serpentine, it is the weaker granite that has been eroded to form the few coves and valleys in the south of the Lizard at **Cadgwith**, **Poltesco** and **Kennack Sands**. The serpentine itself is so tough, it is virtually the same surface that formed the sea bed so many millions of years ago. This accounts for the table top flatness of **Goonhilly** and **Lizard Downs**. We know the Lizard was once submerged because gravels and typical sea-bed deposits still exist on top of the serpentine at **Crousa Down** 100 metres above the present sea level. These have been extensively quarried by man. It is this flat surface that attracted the air force to build the airfield at **Predannack** and the wide, uninterrupted sky that attracted British Telecom to build **Goonhilly Earth Station**.

There are few places in the country that can claim such a varied landscape within such a small area. Much of the Lizard is designated as an area of outstanding natural beauty and many of the habitats are protected as national nature reserves.

ONE PLACE . . . FOUR SEASONS
The LIZARD PENINSULA

Britain's most southerly peninsula is an area of outstanding natural beauty, from the dramatic cliffs of Kynance to the tranquillity of the Helford River.

Write or phone for your FREE map, guide and accommodation list to:-
Lizard Peninsula Tourism Association,
The Lizard, South Cornwall TR12 7NR
Dial-A-Brochure: (01326) 565976 Web address: www.lpta.co.uk

Please mention this guidebook when replying to advertisements

Wildlife

The Lizard has a typical maritime climate, characterised by wet mild winters and cool summers. As a result of this mild climate many sub tropical plants are able to grow here that would not survive further north in Britain. The Helford River has two internationally famous gardens on its north bank - the National Trust garden at **Glendurgan** and the garden at **Trebah**. The mildness of the climate allows crops to mature early with many plants blooming at Christmas. It is not simply the southerly latitude of the Lizard that makes the climate so mild. The warming effect of the sea that surrounds the peninsula has an even greater influence. The particular mechanism involved is the *Gulf Stream*, a sea current that distributes warm water from the equator to the western coasts of Europe.

Ciliate Rupture-wort found only on the British mainland at Lizard Point. Dried & taken with wine or as an infusion, it was thought to cure rupture hence its Latin name Herniaria Vulgaris. *Also said to be efficacious on gonorrhorea & festulous ulcers, especially the sort that are foul & spreading.*

This means that sea temperatures stay within a relatively warm and narrow range throughout the whole year. The beneficial and dramatic stabilising effect of the Gulf Stream on the climate can be gauged from the fact that Newfoundland lies on a similar latitude to Cornwall, about 50° north of the equator, yet winter temperatures in Newfoundland barely rise above freezing. On the Lizard frosts are unusual.

The wild plants of the Lizard are more typical of species found on the Atlantic coasts of Spain and Portugal and it has been suggested that they may be a survival of plants that grew on the original Normannian continent that 'crashed' into Cornwall 375 million years ago. The majority of the wild areas of the Lizard are on the serpentine rock because it only produces poor soils for agriculture. The serpentine supports an unusual community of plants and animals. It is very

The green winged orchid

poorly drained and tends to form permanent and semipermanent standing pools of water after rain. This creates a perfect environment for reptiles and amphibians and much of the downs and cliffs are of national importance in this regard. Some species have adapted to exploit the temporary pools on the downs. Frogs and toads will often spawn before Christmas to allow their young to grow before the ponds dry out in early summer. Britain's only venomous snake, the adder thrives on the heath and they can often be seen basking in the sun near pools.

The mineral composition of serpentine includes large amounts of magnesium from one of the constituent minerals - olivine. The magnesium rich soil supports a community of plants more often found on bedrocks such as chalk, which is also rich in magnesium. Orchids thrive on the cliffs at above **Mullion** and **Predannack**. The National Trust graze hardy

Soay sheep and Shetland ponies on the cliffs to keep down the bracken and gorse that would otherwise strangle the delicate orchids. They perform the job once done by indigenous wild ponies called Goonhillies, now unfortunately extinct.

The seas and reefs around the Lizard are also rich in wildlife. Grey seals breed in the deep caves west of **Lizard Head**. They spend most of their lives at sea but come inshore to moult and breed. September and October are the main breeding months. The pups are born in deep and secluded sea caves. The cows are able to give an exceptionally rich milk that allows the pups to gain nine

The National Trust plays a vital part in conserving the coastal habitat of the Lizard. Soay sheep and Shetland ponies help to keep down bracken & gorse.

kilos in the first week after birth. The main danger to the pups is a storm because even the deepest cave is not above the highest storm tides. After three weeks the pup is abruptly deserted by its mother and over the next two weeks it lives off its fat whilst its sea coat grows. At this time the cows will mate again as there are a convenient number of bulls to choose from, but the fertilised egg will be not develop until spring. The bulls are more conspicuous than the cows because of their darker coats and larger size. They look a bit like sumo wrestlers because of the luxurious rolls of fat around their necks. The males will grow up to 2.5 metres long and live up to about 25 years. The females grow up to 1.8 metres long and live for up to 35 years. The seals will return to the caves in

Cornish heath.

January and February to moult and allow their new sea coats to grow. Seals are easiest to spot between **Lizard Point** and **Kynance** and a smaller number breed west of **Porthleven**. Boats from **Mullion** make special trips to watch the seals.

Dolphins are also seen from the cliffs usually in pods of 30 or 40 individuals following shoals of mackerel and mullet. They make the task of swimming look less like a chore and seem more like a party. The sight of a pod of dolphins will undoubtedly make your day. There is no single place where you are guaranteed to see dolphins and the frequency of sightings can vary tremendously from year to year, but it is surprising what you can see from the cliffs if one simply stops, sits down and looks.

Another large and impressive animal regularly sighted from the cliffs in summer is the basking shark, easily identified by their twin black fins and their lugubrious style of swimming. An adult will grow up to 15 metres long and often come in very close to the cliffs trawling the inshore waters for planckton released from barnacles, mussels and other crustaceans. Basking sharks are extremely docile - they spend most of their lives in solitude but in 1998 there was a large and unusual gathering of over 100 off **Lizard Point**.

The People of the Lizard

The arrival of people on the Lizard is a comparatively recent event in the history of the peninsula. The first people we can say definitely lived here were the *Mesolithic Stone Age* people (7,000-4,000BC). We think they lived nomadically, gathering food from the wild and hunting wild animals, probably similar to the way in which the native America Indians of the 19th century lived. We know of their existence from the discovery of concentrations of flint and chert arrow heads that litter their temporary camps. **Croft Pascoe Pool**, just south of **Traboe Cross** is thought to have been a summer camp site. It was during the later *Neolithic Stone Age* period that these people acquired the skills of agriculture. Neolithic pottery has been found in **Crane Carrick Crags** near **Lowland Point** (section 6) suggesting the rocks may have had some ritual or religious significance. We know that even in the Neolithic period there was a sophisticated trade and exchange of goods on a regional level. Pottery found throughout Cornwall is often found to be composed of clay from the gabbro rock exposed between Porthoustock, Coverack and Kennack Sands. Some pots containing this clay have been found as far away as Brittany. The same rocks are still valued today, but now they are worked for road stone to surface Cornwall's roads.

It was only in the late Neolithic and early *Bronze Age* (2,500-700BC) that permanent settlements and farming became really established on the Lizard. The area around St Keverne was probably first cultivated at this time and some of the existing stone field boundaries may date from this period. Even today, this area retains many hedges having escaped the worst excesses of hedge clearance in this century. This gives the area much of its outstanding beauty as the hedges provide a haven for wild plants and animals (see Walk 6).

Ever since the economy of the Lizard has been based around the twin activities of farming and fishing. The rich schist and gabbro soils making the Lizard the garden of Cornwall. Diversification has never been more relevant with incomes from farming falling and set to decline further as production subsidies are withdrawn. Environmental management and the financial incentives associated with it, are becoming an important source of income for farmers and this is especially true of the Lizard with its rare habitats. The cultivation of bulbs and cut flowers are also important. The mild climate here gives an advantage over northern areas by bringing blooms on more quickly and therefore gaining a premium price in New Covent Garden flower market in London.

Small fishing communities take advantage of every valley for shelter against the sea and storms but with no harbour big or safe enough to hold large fishing vessels most of the trade is conducted from Newlyn on the other side of Mount's Bay. Boats still work from **Porthleven** and **Coverack**, but fishing has declined from the days when millions of pilchards might be caught in one day and pressed in the pilchard palaces at **Porthallow**, **Church Cove** and **Cadgwith**. Today, small boats work the coastal reefs and ledges for crab and lobster.

The National Trust publish a number of helpful & informative leaflets in their *Coast of Cornwall* series

Relevant to this area leaflet No. 12 - 'Loe Pool & Gunwalloe', No. 13 'The Lizard, West Coast, No. 14 'The Lizard - Kynance, Lizard Point & Bass Point', No. 15 'The Lizard, East Coast' & No.16 'The Helford River'.

1. Helston, Porthleven & Loe Bar

The Tripolitania *wrecked on Loe Bar, Boxing Day 1912.*

This first part of the coast is dominated by the four kilometres of chert and flint shingle that make up Loe Bar. Within historic times the Bar has grown to block the small estuary of the River Cober which flows through Helston from the granite moors of Carnmenellis, five kilometres to the north. The ferocity of the sea on this part of the coast has to be seen to be believed. The waves are bigger than those that hit Land's End. In a severe storm the waves will break onto the town clock tower at Porthleven, completely obscuring it. The unusual height of the waves is probably related to the nature of the sea-bed in Mount's Bay. The waves seem to pile up to a great height off the bar and hit the land with tremendous force. Many thousands of tons of shingle can moved in a single night changing the level of the bar by as much as two metres. Even on an otherwise calm day there maybe a strong ground sea running which will throw unexpectedly large waves onto the bar. A number of lives have been lost in recent years by people being washed off the outer arm of the pier at Porthleven or dragged into the sea by freak waves. The best advice is simply to admire the sea from a distance and keep back from the sea edge in this area.

Helston

Helston has always been intimately linked with the Lizard Peninsula. It is the nearest large town and has a wider range of facilities than can be found in Mullion or at Lizard village. One of the best facilities available to the visitor is the **Blue Anchor** in Coinagehall Street. It brews its own beer - the famous *spingo*, reputedly only sold in half pint measures to strangers lest it leave them speechless and trembling with its potency. The Helston Folk Museum is a little gem. It is housed in the old buttermarket and lined with old carts, a huge timber cider press and packed full of archaeological finds from the Lizard. Each May on Flora Day the town dances from dawn to dusk in the famous celebration of spring.

Porthleven

Thankfully Porthleven does not have the ossified prettiness of some other small Cornish harbours and is still very much a working place. Small boats work local reefs for lobster and crab and hand line for mackerel. Fresh fish is readily available in the shops, restaurants and pubs that line the harbour. The village has something of a reputation as a creative oasis. Porthleven Pottery is known all over Cornwall and craft shops operate from the old sail lofts.

Loe Bar

Magnificent stretch of shingle beach. Accessible from a number of small National Trust car parks that dot the cliffs above the bar.

1. Helston, Porthleven & Loe Bar

Flora Day in Helston

On Flora Day Helston is decorated with green branches and flowers in celebration of the arrival of spring. The towns people, dressed in their best top hats and frocks, dance in & out of each others houses behind the town band beating out the *furry dance*. Try to arrive early as the town rapidly fills up and it is difficult to find anywhere to park. First dance starts at 7am & the main dance is at midday. Don't miss the Hal-an-Tow, a re-enactment of St George's fight with the devil that processes around the town. It leaves the Guildhall at 8am. Flora Day is held every year on the 8th May (except where that falls on a Sunday or Monday).

The children of Helston dance past the Guildhall on Flora Day.

The inner basin of Porthleven Harbour

- Post office
- Cafe/refreshments all year
- Cafe/refreshments - seasonal
- Ship Inn Pub
- P Car Park
- P Car Park 1-5 cars only
- T Toilets
- Footpath (not necessarily right of way)
- Recommended footpath
- Track/private road
- Minor Road
- Main Road
- Primary Road
- 0 Scale 1km

Loe Bar & Pool

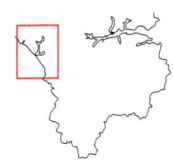

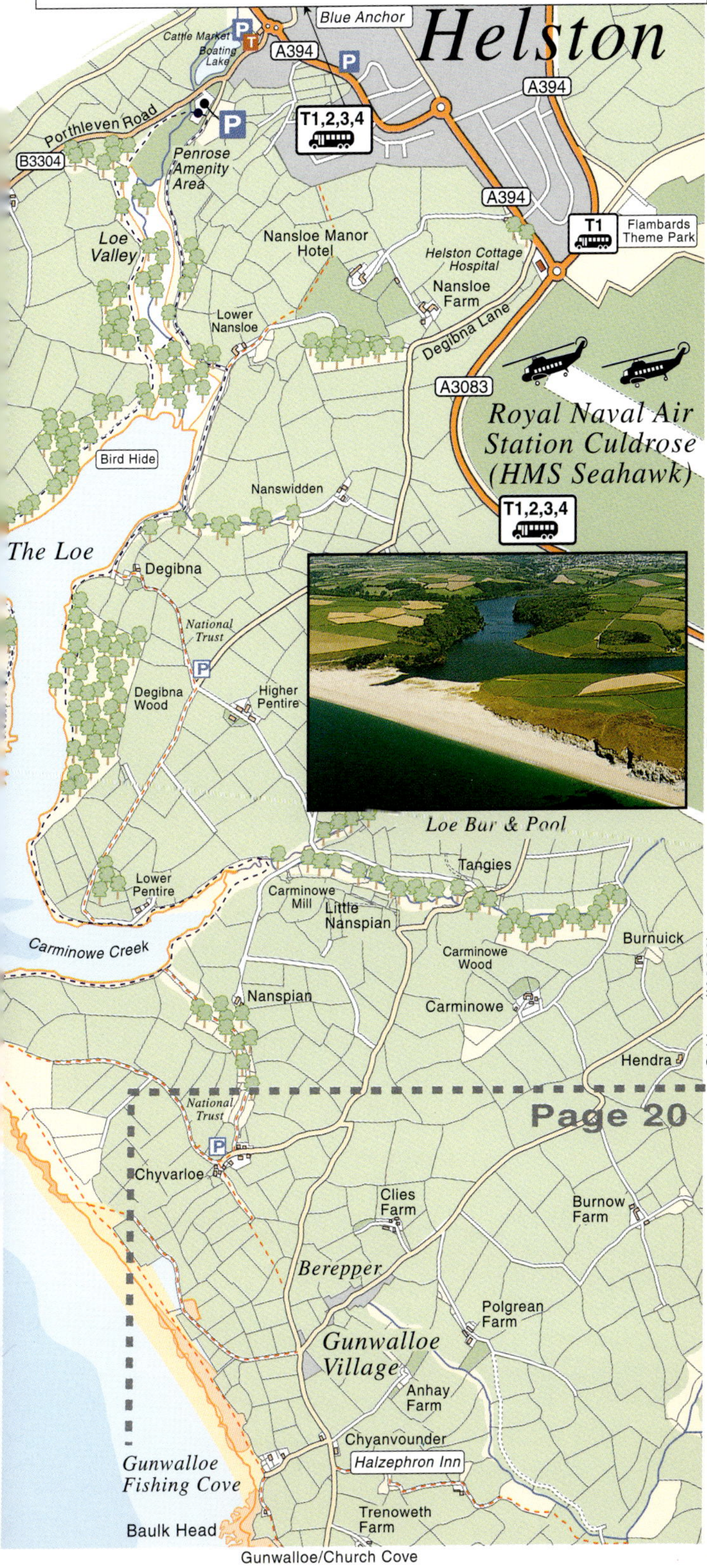

1. Helston, Porthleven & Loe Bar

Walk 1. Circular walk around Loe Pool

You can choose a walk to match the weather. There are a number of small National Trust car parks dotted around the banks of Loe Pool. Smaller sections are within easy reach whether you would like a coastal walk or a walk along the more sheltered banks of Loe Pool itself. There is a resident population of ducks and swans on the pool and they are joined by other birds that over winter here.

For more detailed information about Loe Pool see the National Trust *Coast of Cornwall* leaflet No. 12 - 'Loe Pool & Gunwalloe'.

Distance: 8 km/5 miles round the edge of Loe Pool (4 hrs).
Going: Easy, especially along the west bank which follows the old driveway to Penrose House.
Pub/Refreshments: Nothing directly on the route of this walk, but there are pubs and cafes in Porthleven & at Halzephron above Gunwalloe Fishing Cove.
Best time of year to visit: During any storm to watch the huge waves that crash onto Loe Bar.
Points to look out for: Yellow horned poppy growing on sand bar flowers in May.

Loe Bar & The Anson Memorial

This part of the Cornish coast has claimed more than its fair share of wrecks, often driven into Mount's Bay and onto Loe Bar by violent winter storms. The shingle of Loe Bar, which one might think to be the least dangerous of places to be wrecked, has in fact been one of the most cruel and deadly. Sail ships driven by the south westerly gales would run for cover into Mount's Bay and let out the anchor in the hope of riding out the storm. If the cable parted the ship would be driven stern first into the cliffs or taken up by the huge waves that focus on Loe Bar and literally dumped on the shingle, breaking the back of the ship. What makes it especially cruel is that often dry land and safety were only a few metres away. Onlookers were only able to stand by as a ship disintegrated before their eyes and seamen where dragged out to sea by the strong undertow that occurs here. On one such occasion in 1807 the Royal Navy frigate, *HMS Anson* was wrecked on Loe Bar and was lost with all 120 hands. They all drowned within hailing distance of the shore so that onlookers could hear their cries for help but were powerless to save them. Several local men exasperated by the situation attached ropes to their waists and waded into the surf in a vain attempt to reach the ship only to be beaten down by the waves and barely escaping with their own lives. They were drawn back to shore half drowned.

One of the people who witnessed this wreck was a Helston man called Henry Trengrouse. He vowed to find a way to help prevent disasters like the *Anson*. In time he invented a rocket apparatus that was able to carry a line aboard a stricken ship, allowing people to be brought ashore by a chair and pulley system. Since then it has saved many hundreds of lives. Only in the last few years with the use of search and rescue helicopters has it become redundant. The helicopters that patrol this part of the coast operate from RNAS Culdrose often passing over the site of the wreck of the Anson on their way to and from their base.

2. Gunwalloe, Poldhu & Mullion

This part of the coast has almost all of the best beaches on the Lizard Peninsula. Everybody will have their personal favourite but **Church Cove** is probably the most loved with its ancient isolated church, sand dunes and legends of lost treasure. **Poldhu** and **Polurrian** are within easy reach of **Mullion** and much favoured by locals. In this area for the first time the slate rocks give way to the schists that start the Lizard sequence of unusual rocks.

Great black backed gull. The largest & most beautiful of the gulls on the Cornish coast. They are the buccaneers of the sea bird world often stealing food form other gulls and preying on young birds. A small colony breeds on Mullion Island and others breed on cliff ledges along the coast towards Lizard Point.

Church Cove, Gunwalloe
Wonderful beach in all seasons. The remote setting of the small church is not unusual in Cornwall where many churches are set in isolated coves away from settlements. In the 6th & 7th centuries a tide of Celtic Christian holy men landed in Cornwall from Wales, Ireland & Brittany to convert the locals. A sacred enclosure would be built on the place where a Celtic saint landed or lived and later a church was constructed.

Jangye-ryn
In the contorted strata of the cliffs you can get some feeling for the power of earth movements that result from *continental drift* (see introduction). These slates were originally laid down in shallow water as horizontal layers. As the layers built up over many millions of years the pressure of overlying sediment turned the ooze into solid rock. Movements of the earths crustal plates has squeezed them into vertical contorted folds.

Slate cliffs at Jangye-ryn
Slates at Jangye-ryn originally laid down in water as alternate horizontal layers of mud and sand.

Earth movements caused by continental drift 'squeeze' strata into ever tighter folds.

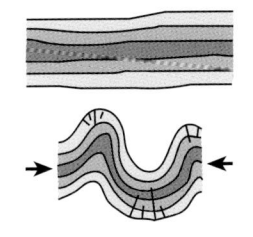

Mullion
The largest village on the Lizard peninsular and with a good selection of facilities including craft workshops and galleries. It is only a short walk to the coast from Mullion and you can take your pick of some of the best beaches on the whole peninsula.

CRíggan MiLL
Mullion Cove
LUXURY TIMBER LODGES

Accommodation ranges from Millstream Lodge B&B to fully equipped self-catering timber lodges situated in a peaceful sheltered valley 200 yards from picturesque Mullion Cove and the coastal footpath.

Mike & Jackie Bolton   Tel: *01326 240496*

2. Gunwalloe, Poldhu & Mullion

2. Gunwalloe, Poldhu & Mullion

Cormorant.
Often seen diving for fish chasing them underwater with strokes of its powerful webbed feet. Oddly for a diving bird its feathers are not completely waterproof and it has to spend some time each day with its wings outstretched drying in the wind. Its cousin the shag is more common and can be distinguished by a crest above the bill and no white markings on the face.

Walk 2. Circular walk from Mullion

There are popular sandy beaches at Poldhu and Polurrian. Polurrian Cove marks the start of the Lizard sequence of rocks. You might think in terms of taking a picnic and including a swim. The dark green cliffs at Mullion Cove make the most spectacular backdrop for a swim (no beach at high water). The walk can be shortened by returning to Mullion along Meres Valley.

Distance: 5km/3 miles round trip (2 hours).
Car Parks: Large car parks at Poldhu Cove, Mullion Village & Cove. *Going:* Generally OK.
Pub/Refreshments: Cafes at Poldhu Cove, Mullion Cove & Village. Pasties at Mullion Bakery.
Pubs: Old Inn in Mullion Village. *Best time to visit:* Spring for the cliff flowers.
Points to look out for: Orchids flower on the serpentine cliffs May to June. Good views on a clear day to St Michael's Mount & the Land's End Peninsula.

First get your pasty in Mullion Village.
The coast path is well marked & used.

Marconi and Poldhu

On the cliffs above the south side of Poldhu Cove and beyond the large Victorian building that is Poldhu residential home there is a memorial to Guglielmo Marconi. In December 1901 the first radio signal to cross the Atlantic was sent from here to Newfoundland and so started the revolution of radio that changed the world forever. The radio station was the forerunner of our modern digital communications now received and transmitted from Goonhilly Earth Station.

MULLION GALLERY
Nansmellyon Road
Mullion
Helston
TR12 7HT
Tel: (01326) 241170

THE Centre for Lizard Peninsula Arts & Crafts

Exhibition and Sale of Work by over 80 local Artists

Please mention this guidebook when replying to advertisements

3. Mullion Cove & Kynance Cove

In this part of the coast schist and serpentine cliffs vie to form the most impressive coastline. Firstly, above Mullion Cove the serpentine forms magnificent dark cliffs. They are quickly succeeded by the high schist cliffs of Predannack Head only to be trumped by the serpentine cliffs of Vellan Head and Rill Point. It is particularly noticeable how the soil above the schist is well cultivated around Predannack whereas the cliffs above Mullion Cove and south of Ogo-dour Cove are left wild because the serpentine produces such a poor soil. It makes this part of the coast feel very raw and remote, a feeling intensified by the Stone and Bronze Age burial mounds that are visible on the horizon towards Goonhilly.

Guillemot. Spends most of the winter on the open sea & comes inshore to breed on Mullion Island spring to midsummer. Mullion Island is the only breeding site on the Lizard. Numbers have fallen in recent years probably due to oil pollution at sea to which they seem particularly vulnerable.

Mullion Cove & Island
Boat trips leave from the harbour in the summer to view the coastline and watch seals. Mullion Island is formed from the lavas that erupted onto the Rheic sea floor 375 million years ago. They represent the uppermost layers in the *ophiolite* (see page 8). It is a breeding colony for a number of species of seabird. Great black backed gulls breed here as do shags, cormorants, guillemots and kittiwakes.

Ogo-dour Cove
This beautiful little cove is a good place to picnic and close to the National Trust car park at Predannack Wollas, The cove marks the boundary between the schists to the north and serpentine to the south. As soon as you climb south out of the cove, you find yourself on the high serpentine plateau of Predannack Downs that stretches northeast to Goonhilly Earth Station and southwest to Kynance Cove.

Kynance Cove
Immortalised as the perfect cove by romantic painters and poets in the 18th and 19th centuries and painted in a thousand pictures. Make sure you arrive as the tide is falling as many of the caves are inaccessible at high water. The serpentine is naturally polished by the action of sea and sand.

MULLION HOLIDAY SHOP

SELF CATERING COTTAGES AROUND MULLION & THE LIZARD PENINSULA. AN EXCELLENT CHOICE OF COASTAL, RURAL, TRADITIONAL & MODERN. 
AVAILABLE ALL YEAR.
CALL INTO THE SHOP OR TELEPHONE FOR OUR BROCHURE & VACANCY LIST. TEL: 01326 240315
CHURCHTOWN, MULLION, CORNWALL. TR12 7HN

Please mention this guidebook when replying to advertisements

3. Mullion Cove & Kynance Cove

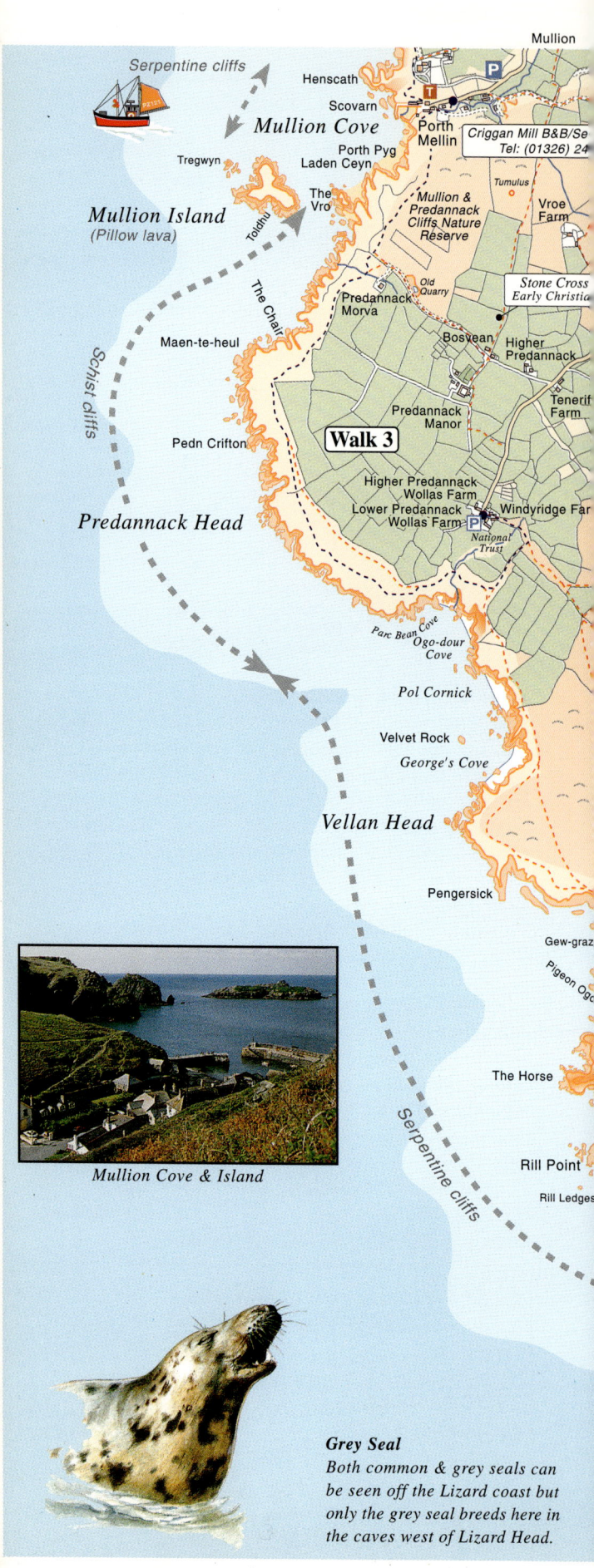

Mullion Cove & Island

Grey Seal
Both common & grey seals can be seen off the Lizard coast but only the grey seal breeds here in the caves west of Lizard Head.

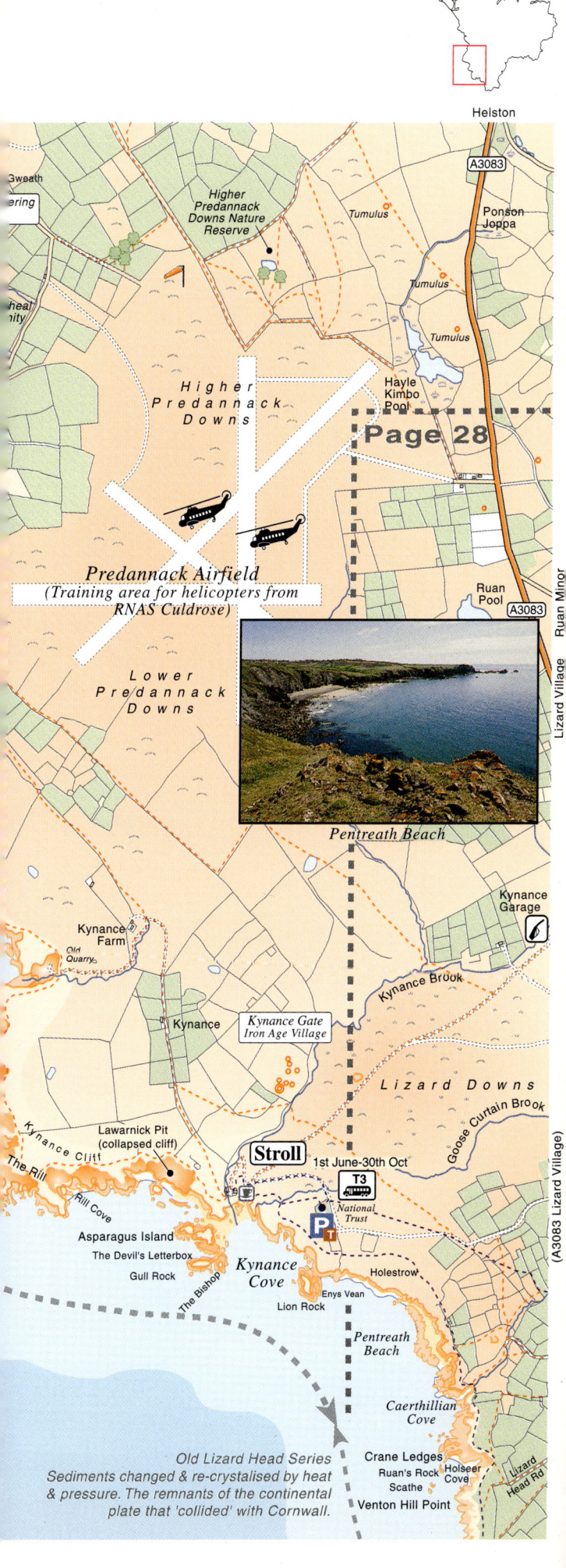

A Stroll around Kynance Cove

Kynance Cove is extremely popular and rightly so because it is great fun to explore the caves and islands exposed at low water. Be sure to arrive at low water though as there is very little beach at the top of the tide. Tide times are published in local papers or you can buy a tide timetable from local shops.

Distance: 1½ km/1 mile. **Car Parks:** Large National Trust car park above Kynance Cove.
Going: A good path follows the river valley down to the cove. At high water you will have to scramble across the rocks at the head of the cove or, alternatively follow the track from behind the car park which arrives at the cafe.
Pub/Refreshments: Refreshments at the car park. Cafe overlooking the sea at Kynance Cove. Take your own pasty from Anne's Famous Pasty shop in Lizard Village.
Best time of year to visit: Spring for the cliff flowers.
Points to look out for: Orchids flower on the serpentine cliffs May to June.

For more detailed information about Kynance Cove see the National Trust *Coast of Cornwall* leaflet No. 14 - 'The Lizard - Kynance, Lizard Point & Bass Point'.

Walk 3. Mullion Cove & Predannack Cliff

This walk takes you onto the serpentine cliffs above Mullion Cove. The cliffs are a National Nature Reserve look out for orchids that flower here in May & June. Ogo-dour Cove is beautiful & rarely busy - a good place to stop for a picnic

Distance: 5 km/3 miles round trip (2 hours).
Car Parks: Large car parks at Mullion Cove. Small National Trust car park at Predannack Farm.
Going: Generally OK.
Pub/Refreshments: Cafe at Mullion Cove. Pasties at Mullion Bakery.
Pubs: Old Inn in Mullion Village.
Best time of year to visit: Spring for the cliff flowers, autumn for the seals.

> From The National Trust car park at Predannack Farm return up the road towards Teneriffe Farm turn either left along the footpath to Predannack Manor or turn left down the farm track at Teneriffe towards Predannack Morva.

Mullion & Predannack Cliffs Nature Reserve

Orchids and other plants usually associated with chalk downs flourish on the serpentine soils.
> Follow the coast path to Predannack Head & Ogo-dour Cove. Return to Predannack Wollas farm & the road.

HOUSEL BAY
Hotel & Restaurant
The Lizard

Stylish a la Carte Restaurant
Lunchtime & Evening Snacks in Panoramic Bar
Spectacular Location on Cornish Coastal Path

England's Most Southerly Hotel

Telephone (01326) 290417

AA***   ETB Highly Commended

Please mention this guidebook when replying to advertisements

4. Lizard Point & Cadgwith

Like its western counterpart Land's End, Lizard Point is exposed to the south westerly storms that spin and spiral north from the Equator in the winter. Countless ships have been driven before the storms and wrecked on the reefs that snake out to sea from Lizard Point. Just how many ships have been lost here over the centuries no one will ever know, but over 500 have been documented in the last 400 years. The rocks of the reefs off Lizard Point are extremely tough and are thought to be the only visible outcrop of the Normannian plate whose collision with 'Cornwall' 375 million years ago caused the Lizard rocks to be thrust from the sea floor to the surface.

The position of Lizard Point as the most southerly landfall for ships arriving from the Atlantic has meant that even from the dawn of historic times the Lizard has been a prominent landmark. It is mentioned by the Greeks 2,000 years ago as West Cornwall was an important source of tin and copper in the ancient world. St Michael's Mount and the Helford river were the main trading centres. In more recent times it has been a centre of communications firstly with the maritime telegraph station at **Bass Point** and later with the radio station at **Poldhu**. The tradition continues now with **Goonhilly Earth Station**.

Cadgwith

Cadgwith is the quintessential Lizard village - self reliant and resilient. The thatched roofs of the houses in the cove are testament to the battering Cadgwith can get in the winter. The roofs are held down by chains weighted with boulders. The local pub is known throughout West Cornwall for the singing of Cornish songs on a Friday night and the consumption of much beer. Just south of the village is the **Devil's Frying Pan** - a massive hollow in the cliffs resulting from the collapse of a sequence of caves.

Stroll. A circular stroll to Carleon Cove

This pleasant stroll through a rare area of woodland follows the valley down to the ruins of the old serpentine factory in Carleon Cove. Extending the walk along the cliffs in either direction will bring you to beaches & pubs.

Distance: 1½ km/1 mile round trip (¾ hour) *Going:* Good.
Bus: T1 stops at Ruan minor, T3 stops at Ruan Minor & Kuggar. *Pub/Refreshments:* Seasonal cafe at Kennack Sands & Cadgwith. Pubs at Cadgwith & Kuggar.

The National Trust publish a helpful & informative leaflet covering this area in their *Coast of Cornwall* series - No. 15 'The Lizard, East Coast'.

From the car park either follow the track straight ahead past the buildings or return a few metres back up the road to the circular footpath through the woods.

PENMENNER
HOUSE HOTEL

Small, friendly & relaxed family run hotel.
Situated just off coastal path.
Stunning sea views.
Comfortable en suite rooms

Non smoking

Penmenner Road, The Lizard, Cornwall. TR12 7NR
Tel: 01326 290370

Please mention this guidebook when replying to advertisements

4. Lizard Point & Cadgwith

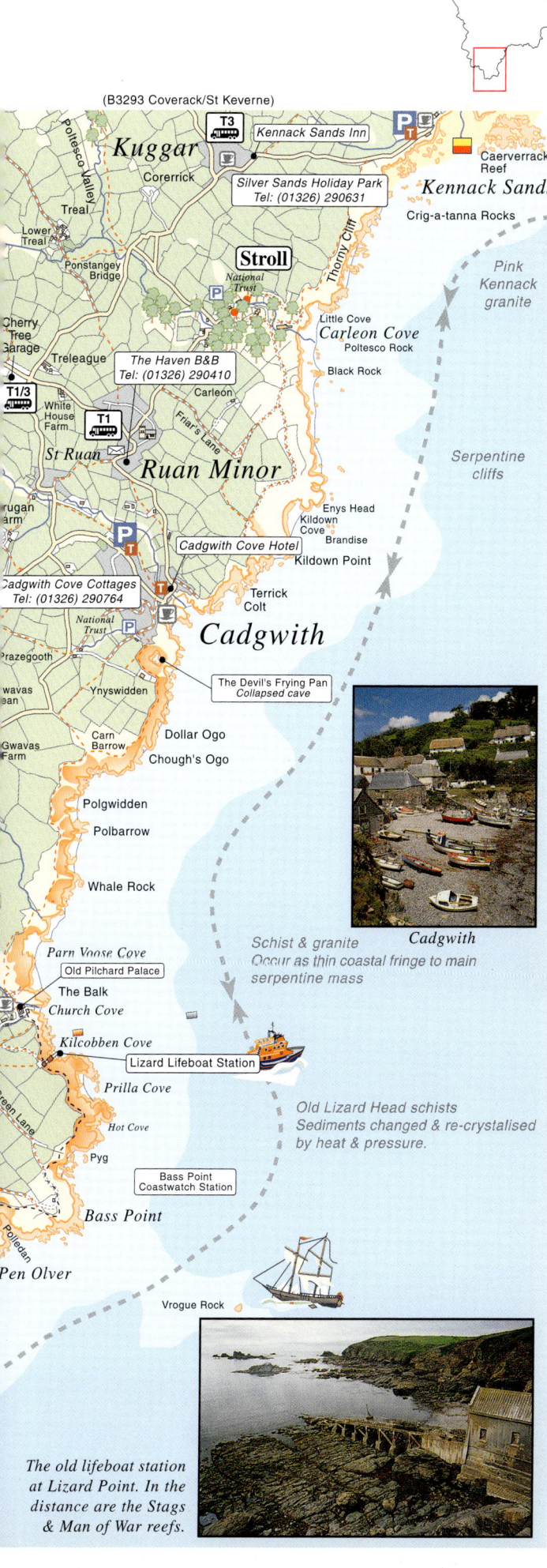

4. Lizard Point & Cadgwith

Walk 4. Circular walk from Lizard village to Church Cove

This popular walk starts from the car park in Lizard village or from the National Trust car park above Lizard Point. Best to take pasty and eat at one of the many benches overlooking the sea. When the tide is out, Housel Bay makes a good place to stop and swim.

Distance: $4^1/_2$ *km/3 miles round trip (2 hours)* **Going:** *Moderate* **Pub/Refreshments:** *Cafe & pubs in Lizard village or pick up a pasty from 'Anne's Famous Pasty Shop'. Teas and bar snacks available all year from the Housel Bay Hotel. Seasonal cafes at Lizard Point and Church Cove.*

For more detailed information about Kynance Cove see the National Trust *Coast of Cornwall* leaflet No. 14 - 'The Lizard - Kynance, Lizard Point & Bass Point'.

The path is well sign posted.

Lizard Point
The most southerly point in mainland Britain and a perfect place for a late afternoon or evening stroll. The present **Lizard Lighthouse** was erected in 1752 to replace a failed private lighthouse built by the Falmouth privateer Sir John Killigrew in 1615. Sir John, accused by many of being a pirate thought he could run a good scam by charging passing shipping for the provision of the light. He never made the lighthouse pay and it soon went dark.

Old Lizard Lifeboat Station
This station was in use until 1962 when a more sheltered house and slip were built at Kilcobben Cove near Church Cove (also on this walk). Thus allowing the lifeboat to be launched even in heavy seas.

Bass Point
The **Lloyds signal station** on Bass Point was constructed so that cargo laden ships in bound from the Atlantic could communicate by semaphore flag with the station. The ship owner would then be telegraphed and could relay orders to the captain as to which markets were giving the best prices. The captain would then be able to either sail up the west coast to Bristol and Liverpool, or up the English Channel to London and the continental ports. The red painted wall by the footpath is a daymark and aligns with the building behind and Balk daymark above Church Cove to help ships establish the position of Vrogue Rock.

Church Cove
Balk Quarry has produced some of the most beautiful green serpentine.

CADGWITH COVE COTTAGES

A selection of cottages for 2 to 12 people in this unspoilt fishing village. Wonderful coastal scenery, ideal for peace and quiet holidays, any time of year.

Contact: Debbie Collins, Ocklynge, Ruan Minor, Helston. TR12 7JS
Tel: 01326 290764 Fax: 01326 290600

Please mention this guidebook when replying to advertisements

Shipwrecks around the Lizard

The Suevic *ran onto the Mèn Hyr in thick fog in March 1907. The Lizard, Cadgwith, Coverack & Porthleven Lifeboats rescued 456 of the 524 passengers & crew. The wreck was blown in half & the stern section towed to Southampton where a new bow was later attached.*

The Lizard has been prominent in the history of shipping from ancient times by virtue of its position on the main trading routes to the Atlantic. Sometimes joyously greeted as a welcome landfall after a long sea voyage, but all too often grimly surveyed by many seamen as their graveyard. The whole coast of the Lizard Peninsula is hazardous. Reefs such as **The Stags**, **Man-of-War** and the **Manacles** lie low in the water at high tide waiting to take any ship that ventures too close. Whilst it is undoubtedly true that the people of Cornwall often welcomed a wreck as an opportunity to salvage valuable cargo it is not true that ships were commonly led onto the rocks by false lights. In fact it probably was not necessary given the carnage a prolonged storm or gale would inflict on shipping.

The Hansey, *wrecked at Pen Olver, November 1911.*

It is difficult now to appreciate the loss of life a storm could bring. Severe storms would commonly lead to the loss of hundreds of lives at sea. It was only with the advent of the camera at the end of the 19th century that we get graphic evidence of the cost. Many of the most horrific wrecks occurred in poorly maintained and overcrowded ships and before the establishment of an effective lifeboat service. Even when the early lifeboats were introduced they were simply sturdy rowing boats and were as powerless against a storm as any other ship. It must have taken extraordinary courage for the first lifeboatmen to put to sea in a storm with only cussed determination and raw muscle power to fight the sea.

In many cases the victims of shipwrecks were buried on the cliff top above where they were found. This practice arose because it was impossible to tell which victims were Christians, and therefore whether they had a right to a burial in consecrated ground. More practically, no churchyard could accommodate the terrible loss of life that could result even from a single wreck. For instance, the 120 victims of the *Anson* lost on **Loe Bar** in 1807 were interned above the bar. The 200 victims of the *Royal Anne* wrecked in 1720 on the Man-of-War reef, were buried in **Pistol Meadow** near **Lizard Point**.

Being wrecked does not always end in disaster though. In 1882, the *Mosel* bound for America with emigrants hit **Bass Point** in thick fog. Such was the way she lay that the passengers and crew where able to walk ashore on to the cliffs as if they were disembarking at a port.

5. Kennack Sands
Goonhilly Earth Station

Tregowris/Tregidden
Page 35
B3293
Crousa Common
Main Dale
Roskilly's
Quillets
Little Trevean
Zoar Garage
St Keverne Beacon
Boscarnon
B3294
Twenty Acre Plantation
Little Kistles
Kestlemerris
Kilter
Cowyjack
Crousa Downs
North Corner
Carnsullan
P
Little Polcoverack
Polcoverack
Coverack
Penhallick
T2
Boak House B&B
Tel: (01326) 280608
Penmarth Farm
Treleaver Common
Trevothen
Little Trevothen Caravan & Camping
Tel: (01326) 280260
Little Pednavounder
Pednavounder
Mount Earl
Trewillis
Downas Mill
Arrowan
Downas Valley
Chynhalls Cliff
Treleaver
The Gaider
Zawn Vinoc
Zawn Carce
Butter Cove
Beagles Point
Ebber Rocks
Downas Cove
Wreathe
Meludjack
Beagles Hole
Dinas Cove
Pedn Boar
Hyrlas Rock
The Bees
Black Head
Serpentine cliffs

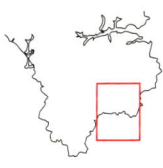

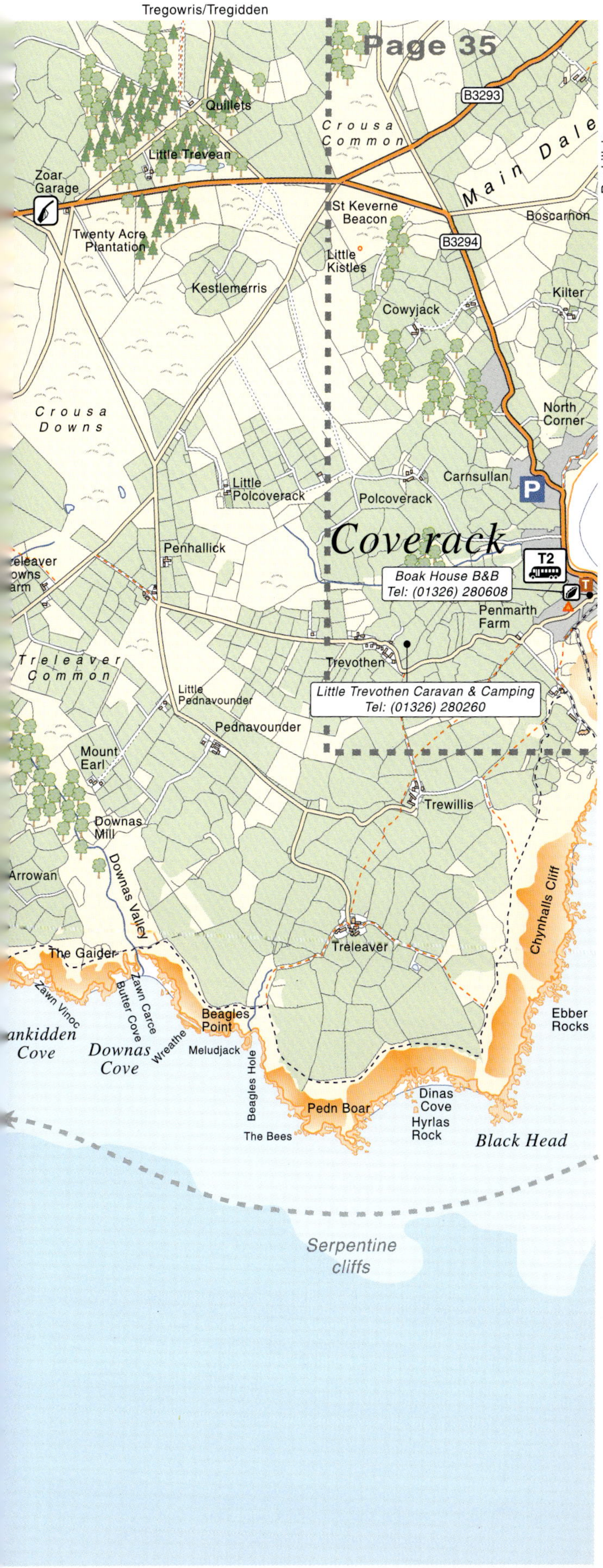

Kennack Sands

Kennack Sands is one of those magical places where childhood memories are forged. It is a combination of classic geological site and fantastically good beach. The wide, sandy foreshore has an unrivalled selection of beautiful pebbles from the different rocks that are exposed in the surrounding cliffs. The predominant rock is the pink Kennack granite that occurs in relatively small outcrops throughout the whole of the southern part of the Lizard. It is always deeply weathered and decomposed forming pockets of good soil on the otherwise uncultivated serpentine soils. Its relative weakness compared with the serpentine means that it forms the broad valleys behind Kennack Sands and Cadgwith. These valleys provide shelter against the winds that whip across the exposed plateau of Lizard Downs in the winter. Just below where the road reaches the beach there are a number of different rocks cutting across each other. It is this sequence that helped to establish the relative ages of some of the rocks in of the Lizard.

Crousa Downs

This area of gabbro is overlain by marine deposits of gravel which were laid down when the peninsula was covered by a shallow sea. The gabbro is famous for the rich soils it produces because it is often very deeply weathered and decomposed. The depth of the weathering can be very irregular sometimes as much as 10 metres deep but also as here very much shallower and strewn with large boulders on the open ground.

Walk 5. Carrick Luz & Downas Cove

This makes a pleasant and undemanding cliff walk from Kennack Sands crossing three types of rock and taking in the promontory at Carrick Luz and the pretty Downas Cove. Although not a long walk it can be easily extended to conclude at the Paris Hotel in Coverack with a pint of beer overlooking the sea.

Distance: 6 km/3½ miles round trip (2 hours).
Going: Generally easy. **Car parking:** At Kennack Sands.
Pub/Refreshments: Refreshments at Kennack Sands.

The coast path is easy to follow.

Carrick Luz & Lankidden Cliff Castle

This promontory of resistant gabbro rock jutting into the bay is the site of an Iron Age (700BC-410AD) cliff castle. It is a natural defensive site and the landward side is protected by a 3 metre high stone and earth rampart. The site was probably fortified as a response to the increasing frequency of raids at that time. It may also have acted as a trading place with ships landing at Kennack Sands.

LITTLE TREVOTHAN

Caravan & Camping Park
Peaceful, secluded site, level pitches
Hot showers/Laundry
Lounge bar/games room
Children's playground

Mrs M Mita, Little Trevothan, Coverack, Helston. TR12 6SD
Telephone 01326 280260

Please mention this guidebook when replying to advertisements

6. Coverack, St Keverne & The Manacles

This area of the Lizard sits on gabbro bedrock. The coast is dominated by numerous small deserted quarries blasted into the cliff face and by two huge working quarries. The gabbro is quarried to make aggregate for roads and for rock armour to protect vulnerable coasts in other parts of the south west. It produces extremely willing soils making this one of the most fertile farming districts in Cornwall. The combination of mild winters and being in the sheltered lee of Goonhilly Downs added to this natural fertility, mean that there is a long and productive growing season here. This gives local farmers the opportunity to get their crops to market two or three weeks ahead of their competitors further north in Britain. They can therefore charge a premium price for their produce.

The rich soils in this part of the Lizard have been cultivated from prehistoric times. Late Stone Age (4,000-2,500BC) pottery has been found in the crevices of **Crane Carrick Crags** and the local gabbro clay was used to make pottery that has been found all over England. This is evidence of a surprisingly wide web of prehistoric trade and commerce. The area around **Lowland Point** is rich in prehistoric field boundaries and the remains of prehistoric huts.

In more recent times the area acquired a reputation for some serious smuggling. The infamous Long Meadow Gang operated from **Godrevy Cove** in the 18th century.

Coverack

Coverack was built on the success of pilchard fishing in the 19th century and although the pilchard shoals have long since disappeared a number of small boats still carry on the maritime tradition by working the inshore waters. A lifeboat was stationed here until 1963 primarily because of the danger of ships hitting the Manacles. The name of the local pub, *The Paris Hotel* recalls the wreck of the *Paris* on the Manacles. Some of the ship was salvaged and now forms part of the hotel. On a summer evening one can sit outside the Paris Hotel and gaze across Coverack Bay to the Manacles as they emerge above a falling tide.

St Keverne

St Keverne is the main settlement on the east coast of the Lizard Peninsula. The church has a memorial to the victims of the *Mohegan* wrecked on the Manacles in 1898.

The Manacles

These rocks are particularly dangerous as they are almost submerged at high water. In the times before the invention of radar, ships would often navigate by hugging the coastline. As a consequence, the Manacles have claimed almost as many victims as Lizard Point. The best view of the rocks is from Godrevy Beach.

Boak House B&B

Overlooks harbour and cove, sea views from all rooms.
Tea & coffee making facilities and colour TV in all rooms.
Home-cooking, children welcome, fresh farm produce, safe bathing, windsurfing, fishing trips, personal supervision.
Contact: Mrs W Watters

Coverack, Helston, Cornwall TR12 6SH Tel: (01326) 280608

Please mention this guidebook when replying to advertisements

6. Coverack, St Keverne & The Manacles

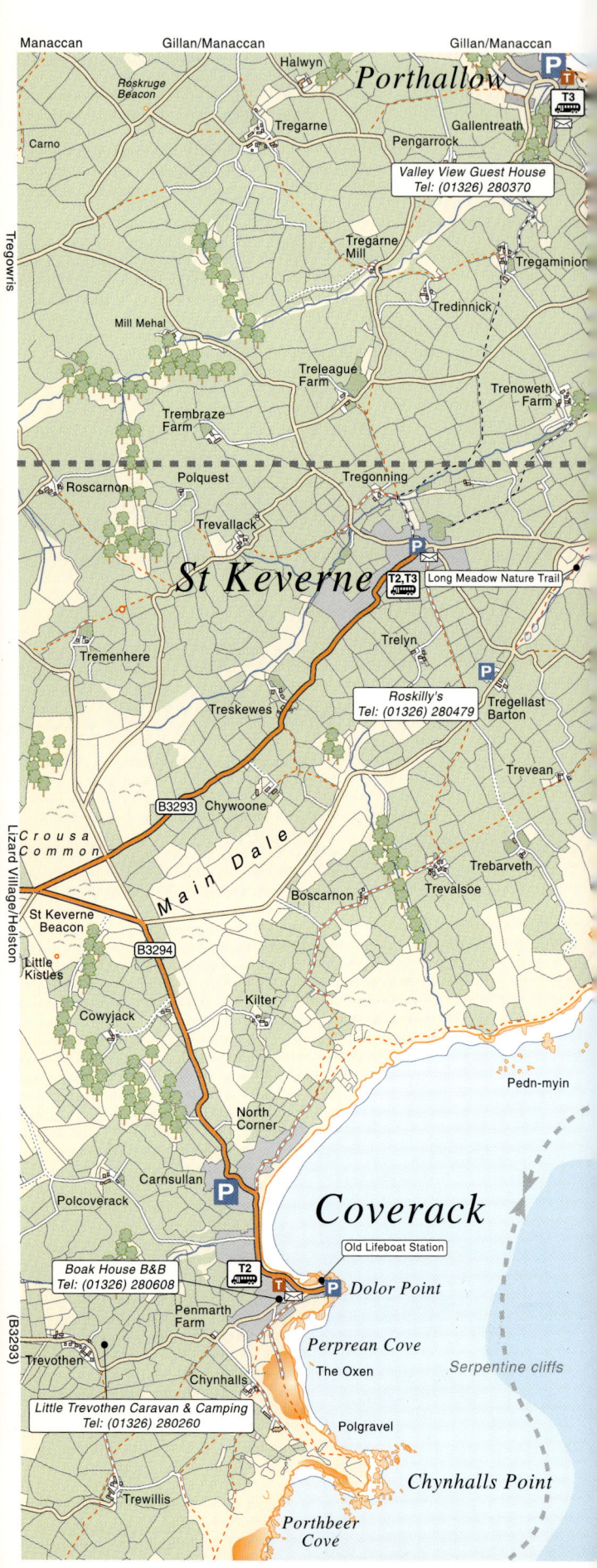

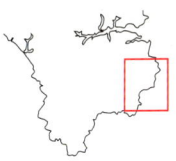

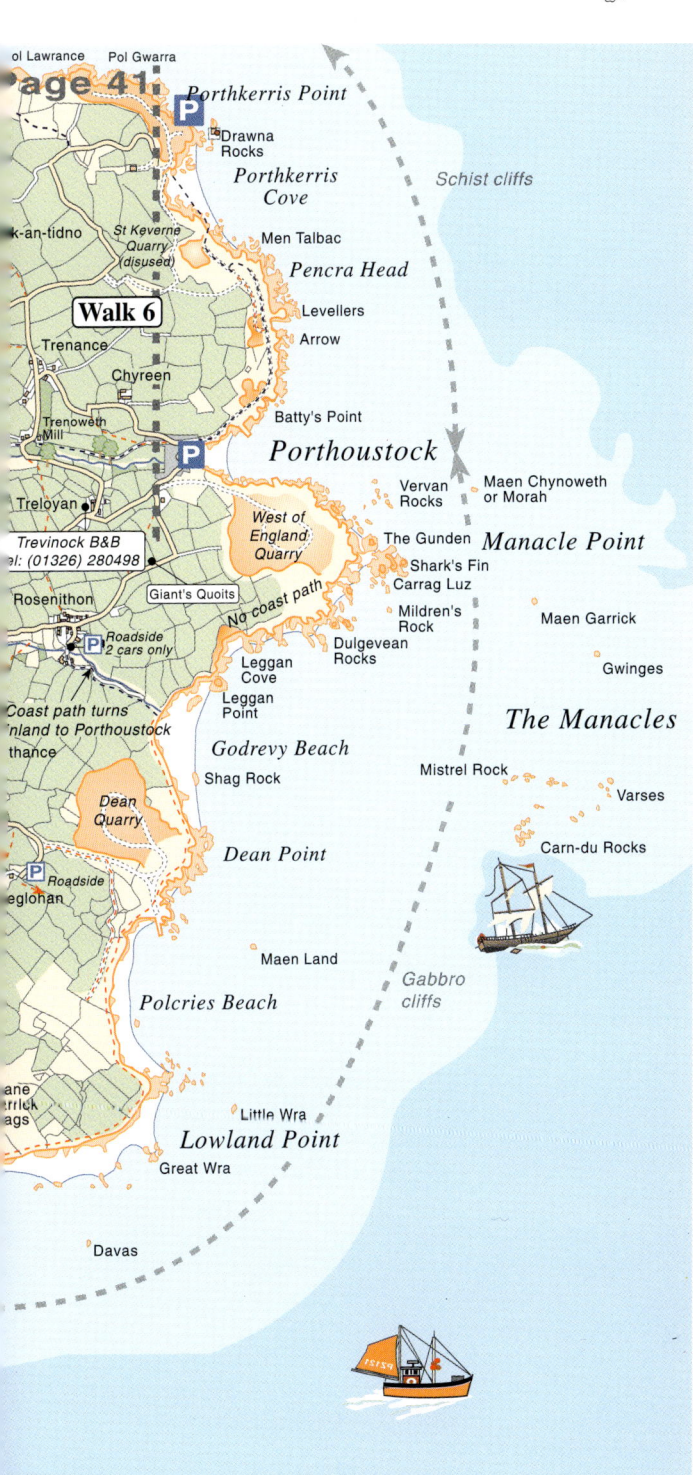

Coverack harbour

6. Coverack, St Keverne & The Manacles

Walk 6. A long circular walk from St Keverne to Porthallow & Porthoustock

You might shorten this walk by leaving your car at Porthallow or St Keverne and taking the bus to your starting point and then walking back towards your car. The section between Porthallow & Porthoustock is dominated by old quarries and would be quite bleak if it were not for the wonderful display of flowers on the cliffs in the spring. A small section of this walk between Porthkerris and St Keverne Quarry is inaccessible at high water. You can stop for a cup of tea at every cove.

Distance: 7 km/4 miles round trip (4 hours).
Going: Some difficult parts on the coastal section involving scrambling over slippery rocks. **Car parking:** Large car parks at Porthallow, Porthkerris and Porthoustock.
Bus: The T3 bus runs between St Keverne & Porthallow.
Pub/Refreshments: Cafes at Porthallow & Porthkerris. Pubs at Porthallow, & St Keverne.

Leave St Keverne Square & walk down Well Lane to the stream. Cross the stream & turn right, follow the path across the fields to the road, turn right along the road for a short distance and then left over the fields to Tregaminion Farm. Pass through the farm & cross the fields & woods to the public road above Porthallow.

Porthallow

Leave Porthallow on the coast path from behind the Old Loft Cafe, walk up the cliff and over the fields to the road. Turn left for Porthkerris Cove. If the tide is high the path between Porthkerris Cove & St Keverne Quarry can be cut off. As an alternative turn right.

Porthkerris

Serves as a base for divers working on the Manacles reef and gives tuition for novices. Cafe/restaurant above the beach during the summer. The cliff to the north has been quarried away to form a platform just above sea level. The MOD observation post was constructed to observe test firing of torpedoes.

If the tide is not too high continue along the beach towards St Keverne Quarry. Walk up the grassy incline & follow the paths through the disused quarries to Porthoustock.

Porthoustock

From the beach at Porthoustock follow the stream & valley back to St Keverne.

Trevinock B&B

EXCELLENT FOOD & ACCOMMODATION
IDEALLY SITUATED NEAR COAST
GOOD WALKS   EN-SUITE AVAILABLE
EVERYONE WELCOME

Trevinock, St Keverne, Helston, Cornwall. TR12 6QP
Tel: 01326 280498

Please mention this guidebook when replying to advertisements

The Helford River & The Meneage
7. St Anthony, Manaccan & Helford

The area that is sandwiched between the south bank of the Helford river and Goonhilly Downs is called **The Meneage** - translated from the Cornish as the 'land of the monks'. This land belonged to the Celtic Christian monastery that was established on the site of the present St Keverne church over one thousand years ago. The steep wooded valleys and narrow lanes are almost a relief after the relentless, exposed downs of Goonhilly. The landscape of the Meneage has a gentle, timeless feel to it. The creeks are best explored from the river. Boat hire is available from St Anthony and Helford Passage - see **Things To Do** on page 6. A pedestrian ferry links the north and south banks of the river in the summer. It runs from **Helford village** to **Helford Passage** and allows you to walk to the National Trust garden at **Glendurgan** and the garden at **Trebah**. There are also good beaches on this side of the river, the best being **Grebe** beach.

Porthallow
Porthallow was a landing station for pilchards caught off the Cornish coast. The Old Loft cafe is in a courtyard building known as a *pilchard palace* where the fish were processed. They were gutted, salted and stacked in huge piles before being sent off to market. This was a very important industry until the sudden collapse of the fish stocks at the turn of the last century.

Manaccan
Manaccan is perfectly placed to act as a base for exploring along the banks of Carne Creek to Helford village and Frenchman's Creek. Starting from here avoids the necessity of driving into Helford village which is often busy in the summer. Manaccan has a fine thatched pub - the New Inn.

St Anthony
Tiny hamlet grouped around the church. Sail and motor boat hire is available from the shop above the beach. The adjacent Dennis Head has fine views across the mouth of the Helford river and Falmouth Bay. It was fortified in Iron Age times and again during the English Civil War.

Helford Village
A prominent port in past centuries. The creek is lined with small quays testifying to the trade that once used the port. In particular the Helford river had a busy trade in tin and copper shipped from Gweek at the head of the river. The custom house at Helford village was intended to collect tax from imported goods such as French rum, tobacco and lace. This was at a time when the majority of trade was carried by ship and when the links with Celtic cousins in Brittany where as strong as those with England. In the early medieval period Cornwall and Brittany shared a common Celtic language and culture.

Valley View House

Bed & Breakfast
Charming house in picturesque fishing cove, en suite available, superb food, evening meal, bring your own wine, warm welcome, on coastal path, sea 100 metres, 'walkers' luggage transfer.

Porthallow, St Keverne, CORNWALL. TR12 6PN
Penny & Ian Hawthorne   Tel/Fax: 01326 280370
Email: hawthorne@valleyviewhouse.freeserve.co.uk

Please mention this guidebook when replying to advertisements

7. St Anthony, Manaccan & Helford Village

Manaccan village

St Anthony-in-Meneage

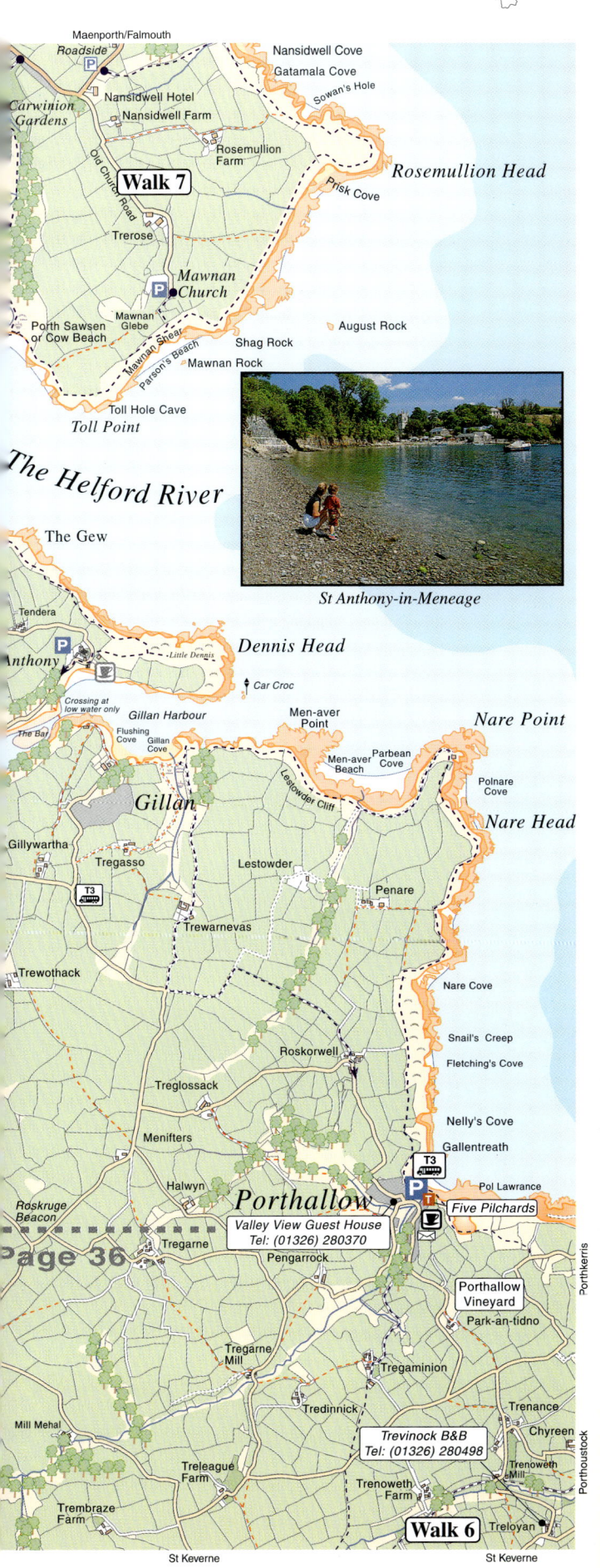

7. St Anthony, Manaccan & Helford

Walk 7. A circular walk to Rosemullion Head (via ferry from Helford village)

The pedestrian ferry from Helford village runs all summer except at low water on a spring tide. Once on the north side of the Helford you are within walking distance of the gardens at Trebah & Glendurgan. Alternatively you might just walk around Rosemullion Head, explore the rock pools at Nansidwell Cove and have lunch at the Red Lion in Mawnan Smith. Best place to swim is the lovely pebbly beach at Grebe. Boat hire available from the Helford Passage for exploring the creeks and quays of the river.

For more information see the National Trust's Coast of Cornwall *leaflet No. 16* The Helford River.
Distance: *To Rosemullion Head - 7 km/4 miles round trip (3 hours).* **Going:** *Good.*
Bus: *The T4 runs between Helston/Helford Passage /Mawnan Smith & Falmouth.* **Car Parking:** *Car parks at Helford village & Helford Passage. National Trust car park above Grebe Beach.*
Pub/Refreshments: *Cafes at Glendurgan & Trebah Gardens. Pubs-* Shipwrights Arms *at Helford Village,* Ferry Boat Inn *at Helford Passage,* Red Lion *at Mawnan Smith.*

> You can gain access to Glendurgan & Trebah from the footpath above Durgan or by following the road from Helford Passage.

Trebah Garden

The famous garden runs down a steep wooded valley with waterfalls and pools stocked with Koi carp. The garden is particularly famed for its tree ferns which were the dominate plant in the Devonian & Carboniferous periods 350 million years ago. Another plant that thrives in the moist, mild climate is the giant rhubarb *Gunnera manicata*. The leaves of which are so large they can be used as an umbrella. Visitors to Trebah are also able to use the private beach at Polgwidden Cove for picnics and swimming.

Glendurgan Garden

The garden was started by the Fox family of Falmouth in the 19th century. They were merchants and shipping agents at the large port of Falmouth which became prosperous as a Royal Mail packet station. Mail and parcels from all over the world were landed here to be taken on to their destination by road. Sea captains brought back seeds and specimen plants from all over the world for the Fox family who are still the main shipping agents in Falmouth. The gardens are at their best in the spring when the camellias are in flower. For information telephone (01326) 250906.

Stroll. A circular stroll to Frenchman's Creek from Helford Village

Best early in the morning or in the evening.
Distance: *2 km/3½ miles round trip (1½ hours).* **Going:** *Good - steep climb out of Penarvon Cove/Helford village*
Bus: *The T3 runs between Helston/Helford Passage & St Keverne.* **Car Parking:** *Large car park at Helford Village, room for 2 cars to park at the end of the road past Kestle.*
Pub/Refreshments: *Cafe at Helford Passage.* Shipwrights Arms *at Helford Village,* Ferry Boat Inn *at Helford Passage.*

8. Gweek, Trelowarren & Goonhilly

The upper reaches of the Helford river are particularly unspoilt and serene. The woods that reach down to the water are ancient and in the past were managed to provide charcoal for smelting tin and bark for tanning leather. The river is only really accessible at two places in this section. Firstly, at **Tremayne Quay** near **Trelowarren House** and secondly, at **Frenchman's Creek** near **Helford** village. Both these places have a secretive feel. The restricted nature of the access to the river is more than compensated for by the quality of the walks. Parking near the path to Tremayne Quay is very restricted but it is certainly worth making the effort to get there.

Gweek

This little village was in past centuries the hub of a large industrial and commercial operation. Even today the quays on the south bank are used by the international sea engineering company Seacore. It first grew in importance because of its role as the port for Helston when the original harbour on the River Cober became blocked by the growth of Loe Bar in early medieval times. The lucrative trade of exporting copper and tin from the mines north of Helston in the 18th and 19th centuries gave Gweek an importance beyond its modest size. The tin trade has been important since at least the Iron Age (700BC-410AD) and there are strategic Iron Age fortifications at **Gear**, **Caervallack** and **Merthen**. The port really went into decline at the end of the 19th century when the tin price crashed and the mines closed. The last great sail ships that docked in Gweek were to carry away miners and their families in the great emigration that followed the decline of the mines.

Trelowarren & The Lizard Countryside Centre

Ancestral home of the Vyvyan family. The stables and outhouses have been converted to provide accommodation for a bistro, pottery, and craft centre and for The Lizard Countryside Centre - see **Things to Do** on page 6. Walks meander through the woods and a path links up with the delightful stroll down to **Tremayne Quay** on the Helford River (see page 46).

Goonhilly Downs & Earth Station

Goonhilly is the mysterious dark heart of the Lizard and a defining landscape on the peninsula. The poor soils that the serpentine bedrock produces have left this area uncultivated by man since he first arrived here 10,000 years ago. Instead the downs are populated by numerous burial mounds of Stone and Bronze Age kings. The ghosts of highwaymen hanged at Dry Tree haunt these moors preying on any person foolish enough to venture across the downs at night. The Earth Station continues the long tradition of communications installations on the Lizard. Pioneered by the maritime telegraph station at Bass Point and the transatlantic radio station at Poldhu.

GOONHILLY EARTH STATION VISITORS CENTRE

- *Visit the Worlds largest operational satellite station on earth!*
- *Purpose built visitors centre.*
- *Fantastic Guided tour including multimedia experience.*
- *Gift shop, family restaurant, hands on displays & film show.*
- *Surf the internet in our internet zone!*
- *All included in one entry price.*

CALL 0800 679593 FOR DETAILS

Please mention this guidebook when replying to advertisements

8. Gweek, Trelowarren & Goonhilly

Dry Tree Menhir. A Bronze Age standing stone adjacent to Goonhilly Earth Station.

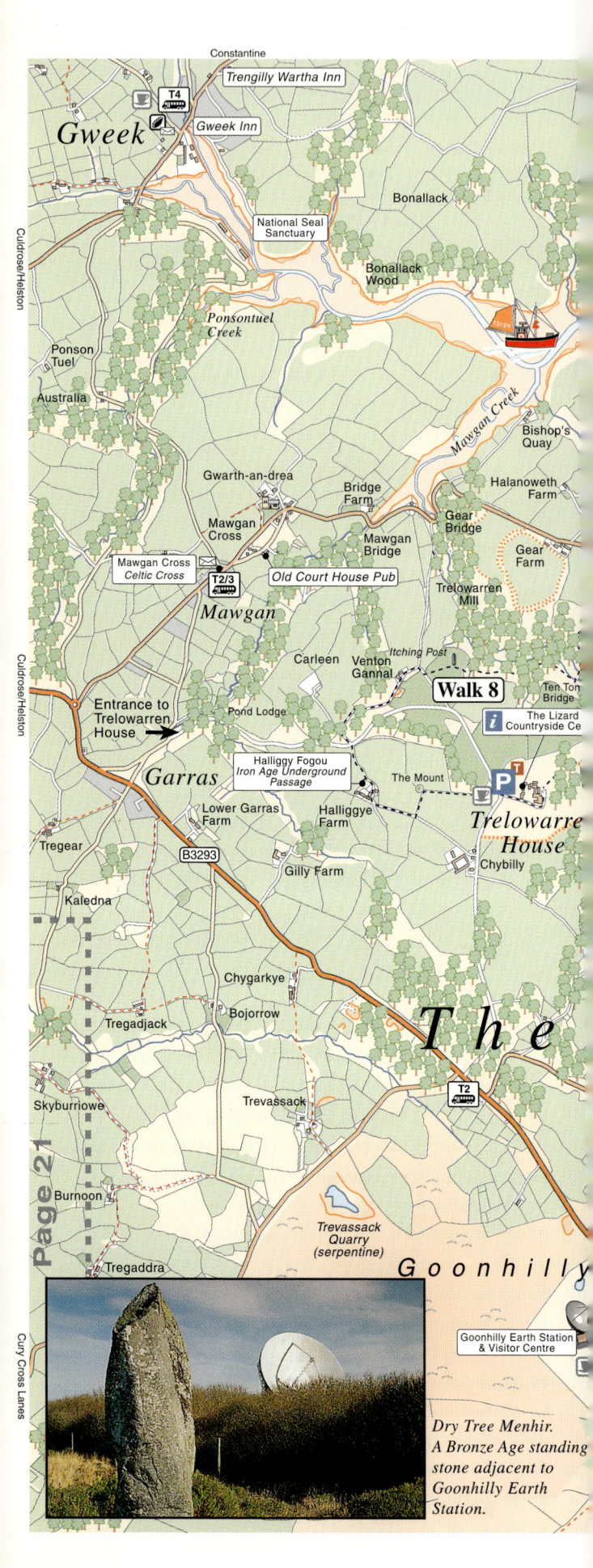

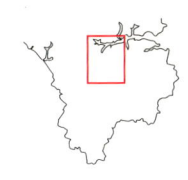

Fishing boat returning to Bishop's Quay viewed from the path to Tremayne Quay

45

8. Gweek, Trelowarren & Goonhilly

Walk 8. Circular woodland walk around Trelowarren Estate

This walk on the Trelowarren Estate is open between Easter and October. The walk to Tremayne Quay is on land owned by the National Trust and is open all year although roadside parking is limited to only two cars. In the season if you want to walk from Trelowarren House to the quay there is a direct route from the house. Picnic areas are provided at the Mount & at Ten Ton Bridge in the woods north of the house.

Distance: 5 km/3 miles round trip (2 hours) - add 2 miles if you walk down to Tremayne Quay.
Going: Generally easy. *Car parking:* At Trelowarren.
Pub/Refreshments: Bistro and bar at Trelowarren House.

Leave Trelowarren House past the plant shop.
The route is sign posted.

The Mount
Good views across the Lizard peninsula towards the west and east.

Halliggy Fogou
The function of a *fogou* is uncertain as archaeological remains have only rarely been found within them. They are generally associated with Iron Age (700BC- 410AD) settlements such as Chysauster and Carn Euny near Penzance. The settlement associated with this fogou is now lost to view but one of the underground passages opens into the ditch that once surrounded the settlement. It is thought that they functioned as cool, underground stores for food but some ceremonial or religious function cannot be ignored because of their relatively complex and large scale construction. Another popular explanation is that they may have been hidden refuges if the settlement was under attack.

Stroll. A stroll to Tremayne Quay

This stroll can be used as a continuation of the Trelowarren Woodland Walk (see above). The land belongs to the National Trust and is open all year. It follows a disused driveway that once linked Trelowarren House to Tremayne Quay on the Helford River. The quay has views over to the wooded north bank of the Helford and has plenty of room for a picnic. Parking is very restricted.

Distance: 3 km/2 miles round trip (2 hours).
Car Parking: Room for just 2 cars at the roadside.
Going: Easy. *Pub/Refreshments:* Bistro and bar at Trelowarren House, pubs at Gweek, Mawgan, Newtown & Manaccan.
For more information see the National Trust's Coast of Cornwall *leaflet No. 16* The Helford River.

Tremayne Quay
The driveway & quay were built by the Vyvyan family of Trelowarren to allow Queen Victoria to disembark from the Royal Yacht to visit Trelowarren. She was unfortunately taken ill and stayed on board instead. The Vyvyan's did get their royal visit when the Duke of Windsor arrived here on a visit in 1921.

Some Geological Terms
More about the geology of the Lizard
Understanding the geology of the Lizard takes a lot of time & effort because clues are only visible in the cliffs & at a number of different locations. It requires a fair deal of investigation to be able to put together a mental picture of the underlying structures in the landscape. In addition to the displays at the Lizard Countryside Centre there are a number of geological collections in West Cornwall which give more detailed explanations of the unusual geology of the Lizard Peninsula. The most descriptive is the Royal Cornwall Geological collection in Penzance. The recently refurbished Royal Cornwall Museum in Truro has galleries with an outstanding collection of minerals & rocks. All are open weekdays and Saturdays.

Basic Types of Rock
There are three main categories of rock. It is not always easy to tell them apart as most rocks can be found in a variety of colours and textures e.g. red & green serpentine.

Igneous rock
A rock that has cooled from a molten state. Slow cooling rocks that solidify underground have a large crystalline structure e.g. granite or gabbro. Those igneous rocks that cool rapidly by, for instance being erupted onto the sea bed, have a fine structure e.g. basalt.

Sedimentary Rock
A type of rock composed of fragments of older rocks, eroded and then deposited by water or wind e.g. sandstone. Also rocks formed from the debris and skeletons of animals e.g. chalk. Often seen in the top layer of oceanic crust.

Metamorphic Rocks
Any rock that has undergone change because of the effect of temperature & pressure. Slate is a metamorphic rock that has a sedimentary origin - it started life as layers of mud before being 'baked' into a tougher rock. The schists that surround the serpentine were originally layers of volcanic ash & lava.

Structure of the earth near the surface
Oceanic Crust
The earth's solid crust beneath the oceans. Formed by an injection of molten lava at a spreading boundary. As new crust is formed it pushes aside the cooled crust setting up the movement of continental drift.

Continental Crust
The part of the earth's crust that comprises dry land & the continental shelf. Mostly formed from igneous rocks such as granite but also made up of sedimentary rocks from the erosion of mountains. Where crustal plates collide the 'lighter' rocks of the continental crust override the dense rocks of the oceanic crust.

The Mantle
The rocks that compose the earth between the crust and the core. They are composed mainly of the silicon rich minerals pyroxene & olivine. Serpentine rock originates in the mantle but is only rarely found at the surface of the earth.

Further reading:
Cornwall's Geology and Scenery. An Introduction by Colin M Bristow (Cornish Landscape Publications).
> Detailed but very readable account of the geological formation of Cornwall, including a chapter about the geology of the Lizard.

Earth Story by Simon Lamb & David Sington (BBC Books)
> Wonderfully clear and readable introduction to geology and explanation of the Continental Drift theory.

Rocks of the Lizard

A selection of stones and pebbles from the beaches of the Lizard.

Key to pebbles in photograph
1. Flint and chert from Loe Bar
2. Schist from Porthoustock
3. Gabbro from Porthoustock
4. Banded gabbro from Porthoustock
5. Pink granite from Kennack Sands
6. Green serpentine from Kennack Sands
7. Red serpentine from Kynance Cove
8. Troutstone from Coverack
9. Quartz

Flint & chert
Formed from the silicon rich skeletons of tiny deep sea animals who thrive in ocean sediment. **Loe Bar** is composed of flint & chert.

Schist
Metamorphic rock formed from either sedimentary or igneous rocks which are re-crystalised under intense heat & pressure. The Landewednack schists of **Lizard Point** & **Bass Point** are altered from basalt & volcanic ash possibly by the intrusion of the serpentine. Best site **Polpeor Cove, Lizard Point**.

Gabbro
Igneous rock formed within the oceanic crust and of the same chemical composition as basalt. Similar in texture to granite but darker in colour. Gabbro is quarried for roadstone near **St Keverne** where it can be seen on the coast.

Pink Kennack granite
Metamorphic rock whose origin is unclear. Best site - **Kennack Sands**.

Serpentine
Properly called a *peridotite,* formed from rocks that comprise the core of the earth. Rich in the blue/green minerals pyroxene & olivine which may weather to deep red or green. As a peridotite it is formed under high pressure & temperature within the earth where there is no free water. As the rock comes into contact with water nearer the surface, the peridotite becomes serpentinised & new minerals such as talc are formed (where talc is very abundant it is called steatite or soapstone e.g. at **Gew-graze** north of **Kynance**). All the peridotite on the Lizard has been altered in this way to some extent. The green serpentine is the most favoured for use in ornaments. The dark green/blue peridotite from **Coverack** is the least altered. Best sites - red serpentine - **Kynance Cove**, green serpentine - **Balk Quarry, Cadgwith**.

Troutstone (troctolite)
Rare igneous rock composed of the mineral olivine weathered to red serpentine & white feldspar. Best site - **Coverack**.